PRAISE FOR
The 3 Loves

In *The 3 Loves*, you will discover the essence of the gospel and be inspired to love God, others and unbelievers in a whole new dimension. The greatest lesson you will learn is how to love, and this book will challenge and equip you to do exactly that.

Ché Ahn
Senior Pastor, HRock Church, Pasadena, California
President, Harvest International Ministry

Larry Kreider and Jimmy Seibert are two of my Christian heroes. Both of them inspire me by their sincere love for Jesus and astounding ministerial fruit. In *The 3 Loves*, you will discover the passion that motivates and propels them forward: love for Jesus, love for others, and love for those without Christ.

Joel Comiskey, Ph.D.
Founder, Joel Comiskey Group (www.joelcomiskeygroup.com)

As the kingdom of God increases on the earth, it does so through sons of the kingdom who are extravagant lovers. The apostle John points out that vertical love is not enough; it must also be expressed horizontally. This book will emphasize to you that the simple truth that threefold love is not just a preference but also a must if we are going to live our lives as sons of the King. For the Church to fulfill her destiny, she must be an oasis of love in a hurting world.

Tony Fitzgera
Apostolic Team Leader,

D1004482

The growing number of books addressing "the stuff and substance" of deepening, committed and solid discipling is a joy to observe. The winds of world-mindedness will only be kept "blown out" of the Body of Christ as God's Spirit gives rise to leaders like Larry Kreider and Jimmy Seibert, who bring this book and its message to us so effectively.

Jack W. Hayford
Chancellor, The King's University
Founder, The Church On The Way, Los Angeles, California

We could subtitle this book "Showing the Kingdom." Here is a great and simple book that would be a wonderful gift for the young adult generation that has left the Church in droves and for those within who need their passion rekindled. Buy a few dozen and give them out!

Daniel Juster, Th.D.
Director, Tikkun International

Those with the deepest walk with God and the greatest impact on people have mastered the secret of simplicity. God-like simplicity is not simplistic—it is profoundly deep, but in the things that matter to God. Larry Kreider and Jimmy Seibert share how God took them to that place, and they inspire you to go there as well.

Floyd McClung
Founder, All Nations (www.floydandsally.org)

For too long, the western Church has struggled mightily to teach and preach the gospel in all its complexity—analytically, logically and apologetically. Here it is in its simplicity and power! This book is practical, clear and transformative. Revival is coming to a dry and thirsty land!

Richard Showalter
President, Eastern Mennonite Missions

The 3 Loves is a must-read for anyone who has grown tired of just going through the motions at church. In a time when the Christian faith has been reduced to little more than an hour on Sunday morning and some rules that we struggle to follow, Kreider and Seibert remind us what being a disciple of Christ is all about: intimacy with Jesus, living in community with fellow believers, and a having a heart that aches for the lost. Thank you, Larry and Jimmy, for making the first-century church alive to us again today.

Matthew S. Stanford, Ph.D.
Professor of Psychology and Neuroscience, Baylor University
Author, *The Biology of Sin: Grace, Hope and Healing for Those Who Feel Trapped*

People want to know two basic answers to the Great Commandment and the Great Commission of Jesus Christ: (1) Where am I in being a disciple? and (2) Where am I in making disciples? Larry Kreider and Jimmy Seibert give us the time-tested path to answer those questions with confidence and competence. This book is a restoration of what will always be a light unto our path. You will be disarmed by its simplicity while armed by its seriousness for twenty-first-century spiritual vitality.

Dr. Joseph Umidi
Professor, Regent University

With kindred spirit and passion, Larry Kreider and Jimmy Seibert combine their stories of love for God, others and the waiting world. By their transparency and authenticity, they convincingly incite us to invest our hearts in these loves with many practical illustrations and tools, including a study guide for small groups.

Keith E. Yoder
Founder, Teaching The Word Ministries
Author, *Healthy Leaders*

Larry Kreider & Jimmy Seibert

THE 3 LOVES

The Three Passions at the Heart of Christianity

**LOVING JESUS
LOVING GOD'S PEOPLE
LOVING A BROKEN WORLD**

Gospel Light

**From Gospel Light
Ventura, California, U.S.A.**

Published by Regal
From Gospel Light
Ventura, California, U.S.A.
www.regalbooks.com
Printed in the U.S.A.

All Scripture quotations, unless otherwise indicated, are taken from the
Holy Bible, New Living Translation, copyright © 1996. Used by permission of Tyndale
House Publishers, Inc., Wheaton, Illinois 60189. All rights reserved.

Other versions used are
NASB—Scripture taken from the *New American Standard Bible*, © 1960, 1962, 1963, 1968,
1971, 1972, 1973, 1975, 1977, 1995 by The Lockman Foundation. Used by permission.
NIV—Scripture taken from the *Holy Bible, New International Version*®. Copyright ©
1973, 1978, 1984 by International Bible Society. Used by permission of Zondervan
Publishing House. All rights reserved.
NKJV—Scripture taken from the *New King James Version*. Copyright © 1979, 1980,
1982 by Thomas Nelson, Inc. Used by permission. All rights reserved.
WEB—Scripture taken from *The World English Bible*.
Weymouth—Scripture taken from the *Weymouth New Testament in Modern Speech*, 1913.

© 2010 Larry Kreider and Jimmy Seibert
All rights reserved.

Library of Congress Cataloging-in-Publication Data
Kreider, Larry.
The 3 loves : loving Jesus, loving God's people, loving a broken world /
Larry Kreider, Jimmy Seibert.
p. cm.
ISBN 978-0-8307-5608-7 (trade paper)
1. Love—Religious aspects—Christianity. I. Seibert, Jimmy. II. Title. III. Title:
Three loves. IV. Title: Loving Jesus, loving God's people, loving a broken world.
BV4639.K73 2011
241'.677—dc22
2010035103

1 2 3 4 5 6 7 8 9 10 11 12 13 14 15 16 / 20 19 18 17 16 15 14 13 12 11 10

Rights for publishing this book outside the U.S.A. or in non-English languages are
administered by Gospel Light Worldwide, an international not-for-profit ministry.
For additional information, please visit www.glww.org, email info@glww.org, or write
to Gospel Light Worldwide, 1957 Eastman Avenue, Ventura, CA 93003, U.S.A.

To order copies of this book and other Regal products in bulk quantities,
please contact us at 1-800-446-7735.

DEDICATION

*We dedicate this book to the hundreds of faithful
believers in Christ we have been privileged to work with
who love Jesus, love His people, and love those who do not
yet know Him, and whose faithfulness has changed
our lives and changed the world.*

Contents

LOVING A BROKEN WORLD

IGNITING THE PASSION

Acknowledgments

A very special thanks to Karen Ruiz, our editor and writing assistant, who did a superb job gathering, writing and organizing the material for this book. Also, thanks to Mary Greenwald and Drew Steadman for their valuable assistance.

Introduction

Every individual's walk with the Lord, and each person's story of coming alive spiritually, is powerful. That's why we are going to tell you our stories in this book. Jesus came into our lives, radically changed our worldviews, and led us on our journeys of following and trusting Him.

Although we live 1,500 miles apart in two completely different parts of our country, we have been blessed to have similar journeys with God. We both live in rather insignificant places: Lancaster County, Pennsylvania, and Waco, Texas. We have both been privileged to serve as lead pastors of churches we helped birth and watched grow into congregations of a few thousand members. Our churches have leadership training schools that have taught hundreds of Christian leaders who are now serving in the nations of the world. God has called each of us to lead a movement to plant churches in many nations through missionaries and church leaders sent from the congregations where we have served.

We are very aware that everything that we have witnessed has been accomplished completely by the grace of God and the power of the Holy Spirit. And we are both totally convinced that the greatest catalyst for spiritual growth is keeping our focus on Jesus Christ and His heart for the needs of those around us.

We passionately believe that every Christian is a minister—that the Lord "has enabled us to be ministers of his new covenant" (2 Cor. 3:6). We are part of a community of people who are walking together in the simple values of the Kingdom: loving Jesus with all their hearts, intentionally investing in one another's lives, and loving those who don't know Him. These three truths have brought us together and changed our lives.

We know there is certainly nothing special about us. We are really common, ordinary guys who simply love Jesus and His purposes with a passion. If God can use us, He can use anyone! God wants us to be the real deal; He loves authenticity. Our journeys started decades ago when God spoke to us separately in Pennsylvania and in Texas, and we each simply replied, "We love You, Jesus, and we want to do all that is in Your heart."

Larry Kreider (Lancaster County, Pennsylvania)

Jimmy Seibert (Waco, Texas)

THE
PASSION

1

Our Passion for Jesus and His Purposes in the Earth

How God has used our personal journeys to make us passionate about loving Jesus and others

A few years ago, a group of pastors from a large church in the Midwest visited us at Antioch Community Church in Waco, Texas. As we took them on the tour around our modest facilities, we peeked into the Antioch Training School. We listened in as one of our church-planting couples shared about their experiences of serving in Mongolia and the Himalayas—loving Jesus in the midst of their journey, investing in people, and seeing lives changed.

When we finished the tour, I (Jimmy) said to our guests, "Well, guys, that's it. It's nothing fancy; we are fairly simple people. In fact, we have chosen to spend our time and energy on just a few things: We seek to love Jesus with all of our hearts and to know Him every day; we intentionally invest in people's lives so that they can invest in others; and, we are committed to reaching the lost, whether it is here or around the world. Every year we learn more about these three things, and that is where most of our fruit comes from."

As we walked back across the street to our offices, I saw tears roll down the lead pastor's cheek. He said to me, "You know, I used to be good at those things, too. But fifteen years and several thousand people later, I find that I am good at everything except those things."

Stories like these make us aware that our journey of simplicity and devotion to Jesus has tremendous power. We are not doing anything new; everything that we want to be comes from the straightforward and clear model found in Scripture. We are committed to giving everyone the opportunity to love God, invest in people's lives, and see the lost come to Christ.

God has called us, His Church, to love Him with all of our heart, soul, mind and strength. He has called us to love one another. He has called us to love people who do not know Him. And He has called us to celebrate all of these things in community. We believe this kind of church is the most exciting and powerful thing happening on the planet.

Loving Jesus . . . loving His people . . . loving the lost. We have found nothing else in life to be more rewarding. For both of us, knowing and loving Jesus has been the adventure of a lifetime. It has been more thrilling than we ever imagined. As church leaders for many years, we have purposed to train the next generation to pursue a passionate relationship with Jesus in their prayer closets as well as in their daily lives. We have treasured the privilege of watching young believers grow into what we were all created for: a passion for Jesus and His purposes on the earth.

Jimmy's Journey to Jesus

As a high school student in Beaumont, Texas, I began to realize that friends, athletics and partying were not meeting the deep need in my heart. On Sunday mornings, I would sit in the back of churches, many times after being out most of the night, hoping to hear something that would make God real to me. Sadly, the two or three places I visited were not able to communicate to me clearly how I could know God. By the third visit, I decided to put seeking to know God out of my mind.

But God saw the longing in my heart, and He divinely stepped in to meet my need with the reality of the gospel. In April 1981, while I was a junior in high school, a friend shared with me some tapes about the end times. The man speaking on these tapes gave a clear presentation of the gospel. I had heard that Jesus loves everyone and that He died on a cross, but never before had I heard that I needed to respond to this message. I didn't know that I could know Him personally. Through this man's simple testimony and explanation, I realized that I needed to make a decision.

That evening when I went home, my older brother, David, was visiting from Baylor University. I knew that David had experienced God in college, though I wasn't exactly sure what had happened to him. All I knew was that when he was home he now prayed before meals. That was different.

In retrospect, I have to laugh at some of his prayers. In his attempt to share the gospel with us one Thanksgiving, he prayed something like this: "Lord Jesus, I thank You for loving us and having a perfect plan for our lives. All of us are sinners and have fallen short of Your glory, but if we repent and turn to You, Jesus, then You will save us and make us new creatures. Thank You for this family and for this food. Amen." At the time, I knew he was trying to say something, but I wasn't sure what it was.

When I came home after listening to that tape, I went to David and told him what I had heard. I shared with him what

I understood about the gospel and asked him what he thought about it. Wisely, he asked, "Well, what do you think about it?"

I responded, "I realize this is a big commitment. I'll have to live life differently, and I don't know if I am ready."

David said, "Do you believe that Jesus is who He says He is and that He has eternal life for us?"

"Yes."

"Well," he challenged, "what are you waiting for?"

When he said that, I realized that God was answering my heart's cry. He was inviting me into the divine relationship He had made me for. I prayed a simple prayer with my brother that night: "Lord Jesus, I have sinned against You and others. I want You, and I need You in my life." An incredible peace filled my heart—a peace I had never known before. Up to that point, I had been running from party to party and from achievement to achievement to try to be somebody and feel like I was worth something. But in that moment of simple response to Jesus, I realized I was somebody: I was His son.

My brother left the next morning to go back to school. Before he left, he told me to read the Bible, pray every day, and tell everyone I knew about Jesus. He also gave me a Christian tape by B. J. Thomas called "Happy Man." With that crash course in discipleship, I was ready to go. I started to read my Bible and talk to God, and I tried to share my faith.

What no one told me was that people didn't always like it when you shared your faith. A couple of weeks after my decision to follow Christ, I was with a few friends at our annual spring break beach getaway. We were sitting around fishing and drinking beer as we always had, but Clint, the guy who had shared the tape with me, and I had agreed to be different. We went from person to person, asking them what they thought about God and what they knew about Jesus. The leader of our group began to ask, "Hey, what's your deal, guys? Why are you trying to ruin our time by talking about God? We are just trying to have a good time here. Have you guys gotten weird or religious?"

Clint and I fumbled around and said nothing in response. We were not ready for that kind of pushback. The rest of the week, we backed off and went with the flow, as if nothing had changed in our lives.

For the rest of my junior year and all of my senior year in high school, I did not grow much because I didn't have regular Christian community or discipleship. I kept the same friends, and my days slipped back into their normal routine. It was in the midst of this season that God spoke to me in a way I had never experienced before. God spoke to me in a dream. As I stood in a windy wheat field divided into two parts by a white fence that extended as far as I could see, a voice spoke to me, saying, "I am coming to separate the wheat from the chaff, and no longer will people be able to ride the fence, for they will either be for Me or against Me."

I had never had a spiritual dream, nor did I know that other people did. All I knew was that somehow God was trying to speak to me. Unsure of what to do in response, I simply went on with my life. Before long, this dream became very significant.

In the fall of 1982, I enrolled as a student at Baylor University. My career ambition was to become an influential person who changed the world through business, law or politics. One of the main reasons I chose Baylor was that I had heard there were people there who loved and knew Jesus, and I wanted that, too. I showed up on campus with all of these desires in my heart.

During the orientation, the leaders used a diagram called the "Welcome Week Wheel" to illustrate the concept of living holistically. This wheel had Jesus Christ in the middle, with four surrounding spokes: social, physical, spiritual and intellectual. The four spokes looked great to me, so I dove in with great enthusiasm.

Physically, I began working out and getting into shape. Spiritually, I joined Bible studies and went to church. Socially, I made dating and hanging out top priorities. Intellectually, I worked hard enough to make Bs, but I also honored the words of my mom, who had told me before I left home, "Remember, college is about more than good grades."

Over those first two years, I got involved in a fraternity, leadership opportunities and service projects. I was on the fast track to be somebody. It wasn't that I was a bad guy; I was just doing what I saw around me. My basic understanding was that God loved me no matter what, and as long as I didn't do anything super bad, I would be just fine. I could pursue all my ambitions as long as I added the little phrase, "I want to do all this for God." Though it sounded good, I knew in my own heart that I was living a double life.

Toward the end of my sophomore year, it became apparent to me that I was missing something. By that time I had heard the saying, "You are not really living for Jesus. You are just riding the fence." My dream about the wheat field and the white fence came back to me, and I realized that fence was the dividing line for God. I couldn't live on the fence; I was either going to be for Him or against Him. He was coming to separate the wheat from the chaff, and I wanted to live in the fruitfulness of God. Once I made that connection, I began to say, "God, I want to follow You with all my heart."

I was dating a girl at the time who was a young believer like me. We started searching Scripture together, trying to better understand the Christian life. But as God drew me closer to Himself through His Word, my girlfriend began to drift away from me. At the end of the school year, I went to visit her at her home in San Antonio. It was there that she officially broke up with me. I was shocked and devastated because I had really begun to believe that she might be the woman I was supposed to marry.

Just after our defining conversation, I went jogging. Running down the street, crying out for help in my pain, I realized that I had a choice to make. Pain is inevitable, and as humans, we react to painful experiences, but with every heartbreak comes a choice beyond the initial reaction. We can either respond by drawing near to God or by pulling away from Him. This was an opportunity for me to draw near. That one decision, as much as any decision I have made, changed the course of my life.

As I drove down Interstate 10 from San Antonio to my home in Beaumont, it became clear to me that I hadn't given God all of my heart. So, I began asking Him to help me. "God," I prayed, "I will give You three months to show me who You really are."

I realized that there were distractions—things in my life that were not going to help me know Him. So, I began to get rid of those things. First, I took my chewing tobacco and threw it out the window; it had been a habit since the seventh grade. Then, I took my secular cassette tapes and threw them out the window as well. I didn't want anything to distract me from pursuing God with all my heart. I made a decision not to watch TV or movies for three months, because I realized that I was living my life vicariously through other people. I would see someone on the screen and want to be like him or her instead of looking at Jesus and wanting to be like Him. As I categorically went through my life, I made decisions for that three-month window to make sure that I would connect with God with all my heart.

In Beaumont, I had a job lined up working at a chemical plant eight hours a day. My daily routine for the summer involved seeking God and working. I made a commitment to read a chapter of the Bible, starting with the book of Matthew, every day and to do exactly what it said. In the morning I would read, and then I went to work. I talked to God throughout the day, and whatever I could remember from the words and life of Jesus that I had read that morning, I would apply.

Let me tell you, doing exactly what the Bible says is harder than it sounds. By the end of Matthew 6, I had given away almost everything I had and had forgiven everyone I hadn't planned on forgiving. By the time I got all the way through the book of Matthew, my whole worldview had changed.

Somewhere in the middle of the summer, I thought to myself, *Oh my goodness; I'm turning into a weirdo! All I do is read the Bible and pray.* But the more I thought about it, the more I realized that I had never before sensed God's presence, love and peace the way I was experiencing them then. *Oh well,* I concluded. *If that's what a weirdo is, then that is okay with me. I want to be wholly His.*

On the morning I was to return to school, I woke up at 6:00 A.M. and began to weep uncontrollably. This was not normal for me; I am not an overly emotional person. At the breakfast table, I could not hold back the tears. My parents were obviously concerned and said, "Son, do we need to get you a psychologist? What's wrong with you? It seems that you are falling apart." Though they did not understand my spiritual journey at that time, I still knew that they loved me.

I didn't know why I was crying, so I just responded, "No, I just love you guys. That's all it is." Somehow I convinced them that I was fine, and they reluctantly let me leave.

Driving back to Baylor University, I continued to cry for another hour. I asked God what was wrong with me, and He spoke to my heart: "You asked Me to show you I am real, and I have come!" In that moment, I realized that everything I had wanted, God had given. That summer, Jesus became so real to me. I was forever changed. What I would come to know over and over again in my life is that the simple words of Jesus, lived out day by day in the life of any believer, will not only change that person's life but will also give him or her the opportunity to change the world. The simple values of the Kingdom, when lived out, contain remarkable transformative power.

My heart has been stirred to believe that not only my focus but also my life must be about the simple things of the Kingdom as commanded by Jesus. Jesus said, " 'You must love the Lord your God with all your heart, all your soul, and all your mind.' This is the first and greatest commandment. A second is equally important: 'Love your neighbor as yourself.' The entire law and all the demands of the prophets are based on these two commandments" (Matt. 22:37-40). When these simple values—love God, love others, and love those who don't know Jesus—are lived out radically, it changes not only the individual, but also the people around him or her.

So where are you in your journey today? Is Jesus so real to you that He is a breath away at any moment? Are other people, rather than yourself, the center of your focus? Are you aware that there are people all around you who don't know Jesus and with whom you could share your faith? The deeper things of God are not the edges of theology and doctrine; rather, they are the radical values of Jesus lived out day by day in those whose hearts are wholly His.

Larry Encounters God

I grew up a simple farm boy in Lancaster County, Pennsylvania. As an only son, I spent my childhood looking forward to the day when I would eventually take over the family farm. I was privileged to be raised in a Christian home and attended church every Sunday near my hometown of Lititz. When I was 11 years old, I attended a revival meeting at our church. The preacher spoke about eternal life and the importance of living for God and not spending eternity in hell. That night, I was convicted of my sin, but most of all I remember thinking that I did not want to go to hell. What I really wanted was "spiritual fire insurance." Hell did not seem like an attractive destination, and I thought I should join up, just to be safe. So, I stood at the meeting during the altar call and later was baptized and became a church member. Only God knows what really happened to me during this season of my life.

In retrospect, I think I wanted to live for the Lord, but in reality the commitment I had made lasted only a few months. I went to church every Sunday morning, but I did little to further my initial encounter with Christ, and it wasn't long before I was living a double life. I was a counterfeit. When I was with my Christian friends, I acted like a Christian. But when I was with my non-Christian friends, I acted just like them. Something was desperately missing.

I knew who Jesus Christ was; I recognized that He was God, but I did not develop a relationship with Him. I didn't really know Him personally. I can now see that without a true personal relationship with God, I had a form of godliness that may have looked okay on the surface, but inside I was dreadfully empty. I was like one of those churchgoers that Dr. Vance Havner described by saying that too many church members have been starched and ironed, but they've never been washed. I was not experiencing a spiritual renewal inside of me.

A few years later, I met LaVerne, a cute girl from high school, and started to date her. One night she confronted me with the question, "If you were to die tonight, are you sure you would go to heaven?"

I didn't know, so I responded defensively, "Nobody knows that!"

She said emphatically, "Well, I know."

I felt uncomfortable that night because I was confronted with the truth. You see, I could talk about God and the Bible, but I couldn't talk about Jesus, because I didn't really know Him personally. I imagined (and hoped) that if I did enough good things, and didn't do anything too wicked, God would accept me.

LaVerne was amazing. She acted like Jesus lived in the house with her and drove in the car with her (I found out later that He really did!). She had a certain peace and confidence about her that I did not have. I definitely wanted that kind of peace. And I was really trying to impress her. I wanted to have an ongoing relationship with her. But I knew I was missing something in my life. So I went home that night and opened my Bible.

Suddenly, everything I read in the Bible spoke directly to me. I read where Jesus addressed the religious people of His day as "You hypocrites!" Wow, Jesus strongly disapproved of religious pretenders, and I was one of them! I was a hypocrite. I knew that even though I acted like I had it all together and was often the life of the party, when I went home and was alone, I was not only a fake but I also felt really lonely. I was not trusting Jesus to change me. I did not have a life-transforming relationship with Jesus Christ. I was just a little bit religious.

The conviction of God gripped me that night! I was afraid I would die without God. I finally understood that no matter how good I thought I was in my own eyes or in the eyes of those around me, in God's eyes I was a sinner. At last, I realized that Jesus Christ had died and risen for *me*, to pay the penalty for *my* sins. I knew I had to turn my life over to Him—completely.

That night I opened my heart to Him: "Jesus, I give You my life. If You can use this rotten, mixed-up life, I'll serve You the rest of my life."

Amazingly enough, God took me at my word. The moment I believed that what His Word says is true, I came alive spiritually. I had remembered that John 3:16 says clearly that God so loved the world that He gave His only Son, and whoever believes (totally trusts) in Him will not perish but have eternal life. I believed, and I became a new creation in Christ at that moment. It was an utterly undeserved miracle of God. My attitudes changed. My desires changed. The way I thought changed. I was no longer a phony. I became a real authentic Christian! I had submitted to Jesus Christ as Lord—the King and ruler of my life—and there was no turning back. I had an overwhelming sense of peace. I now understood what LaVerne had. She didn't just have religion; she had Jesus in her life!

I now knew, without a doubt, that it was not enough simply to believe that Jesus Christ lived 2,000 years ago, that He was born of a virgin, that He performed miracles, and that He died on a cross and was raised from the dead. Saving faith took my belief to the point of *knowing* I was made right in God's eyes through Jesus Christ. I now knew *my* Lord was willing to make the absolute final payment for *my* sin by His death on a cross. *My* sin against God required the payment of death, but Jesus Christ became the ultimate sacrifice—the once-and-for-all payment on *my* behalf. As a result, God had given *me* the free gift of salvation just because I believed and received His Son! And God the Father gave me an awesome love for His Son, Jesus.

I came alive spiritually at that moment, and over the decades since He started with me, I have been a work in progress. He is certainly not finished with me. Whenever life seems to get complicated, I remember what is truly important in life, and I say along with Paul, the apostle, "I . . . forget everything except Jesus Christ, the one who was crucified" (1 Cor. 2:2). This is God's message to mankind. It is the message of Jesus Christ, who is the center of Christianity: Without Him, your life and my life are without meaning and purpose. I have found that knowing and loving Jesus just gets better and better the longer I serve Him. It has now been more than 40 years since I received Him as my Lord, and I would not trade one day since that experience for anything in the world!

The next day, when I picked up my girlfriend, LaVerne, at her home, she knew instantly that something had happened to me. Jesus Christ had totally revolutionized my life. I was completely changed. He had become my Lord and King. And there was no turning back. My journey with God had just begun.

In the community of Jesus, there are many stories to tell. You have your own story to tell. Each story is unique and makes a difference in the Body of Christ. Our stories set us on a path to fully live out God's calling on our lives.

My heart has been stirred to believe that our focus must be on the simple things of the Kingdom. As we strive to live out these principles in the context of community, people are able to embrace Christ's vision so that He can be glorified through His Church on the earth. Over the years, I have continued to grow in the conviction that everyone is called by God to live out the simple values of loving Jesus, His people and the lost. But how do we do it? That's what we will discover in the chapters ahead, as we tell more of our stories of choosing to follow and obey Jesus wherever He leads us.

Jesus was once asked to describe the most important commandment. He replied, " 'You shall love the Lord your God with all your heart, and with all your soul, and with all your mind.' . . . The second is like it, 'You shall love your neighbor as yourself' " (Matt. 22:37-39, *NASB*). This command is so integral to our faith that it is called the Great Commandment. Later, Jesus gave the Church a mission statement, calling us to "Go therefore and make disciples of all the nations, baptizing them in the name of the Father and the Son and the Holy Spirit, teaching them to observe all that I commanded you" (Matt. 28:19-20, *NASB*). This is known as the Great Commission.

Most believers throughout history have affirmed the importance of the Great Commandment and the Great Commission, yet it seems that seldom have these truly been our core values. If we are honest, are these central values of Jesus the focus of our lives? We often get complex in our ministry, doing everything well except that which matters most. We allow our controversies, not our central values, to define us. Our journey is one of learning to put first things first—to radically love Jesus, His people and the lost.

Neither Jimmy nor I started out with the intention of being in full-time vocational ministry; we simply were eager to hear and respond to God's call in our lives. We are well aware of the fact that most people are not called to full-time vocational ministry, but are involved in ministering in their workplaces and neighborhoods. You might say, "I'm not a missionary; I'm just a businessman." Well, in God's kingdom, no one is "just a businessman." They are either called by God to business or they are not. If they are, then the Great Commandment and the Great Commission need to be lived out in their business world. The same is true for those called to arts and entertainment, social work, education, construction and every other field. Whatever God calls you to do, that is your place of influence and ministry.

When we really take hold of Jesus' values, and walk them out every day, we cannot help but have an impact on the world around us. As we personally experience His love, presence and power, God brings us into a family of believers who can change our lives. We can take part in transforming the world around us so that His purposes can be fulfilled on the earth, and we can be a dynamic community of people that begins to look like the Early Church as described in Acts 2:42-47. Of course, we won't get it all right, all of the time, but we can start on a path toward seeing God do great things in and through us as we live out the simple values of loving Jesus, loving His people, and loving those around us in our broken world.

2

A Return to Simplicity

**Loving Jesus, loving His people,
and loving a broken world**

One day, as a younger Christian, I (Jimmy) thought about what it meant to truly follow and trust Jesus. God asked me a few simple questions that brought me back to a fundamental truth.

First, He asked me, "Jimmy, who is someone that you know who really loves Me?" I immediately thought of my friend Chris.

"What is it about Chris that shows you he loves Me?" the Lord asked. As I thought about it, I realized that Chris loved Jesus with all his heart, soul, mind and strength. Then the Lord asked me, "Jimmy, can you try to do that?"

"Yes, Lord, I can," I replied.

Then He asked me, "What else do you notice about Chris?" I knew that what made Chris special was not only his love for God, but also his love for others. The Spirit spoke once again and asked, "Do you think you can do that, too? Can you love the people in front of you?"

"Yes, Lord, I think I can do that," I said.

"The whole Law is wrapped up in that simple statement," He reminded me. "You are to love Me with everything you have, and you are to love your neighbor as yourself. As long as you do that, you are always free. You don't have to worry about all the unanswered questions. Simply live out that life of love."

This truth has anchored me throughout my journey thus far. When I have questioned different theological or doctrinal perspectives along the way, I always come back to the simplicity of loving Jesus and loving people. I am always right in the center of God's will when I am doing these things.

Loving people involves loving those who do not yet know Him. As the Body of Christ, we have the task of rising up to take the gospel to the ends of the earth. But it won't just happen. We have to be the people of God, focused on obediently accomplishing His purposes. The question we constantly wrestle with is "What kind of people actually make up the kind of church that will truly take the gospel to all nations?"

We, in the Church, should simply be people who learn from Jesus, make His values our own, and then reproduce those values everywhere we go. We must become what we call *value carriers*: people who take seriously who God is and how He wants us to live. Then, we give ourselves to walking it out and teaching others how to walk it out as well.

In Acts 4:13, members of the Jewish Council were astonished that the apostles were preaching with great wisdom and boldness, even though they were not educated men. These religious leaders recognized that Peter and John had been with Jesus. Isn't that great? They were so caught up in God that people saw them as those who had been with Jesus. That's how the gospel was imparted—by Jesus loving people through those who were consumed with Him!

We want people to be growing in Christ-likeness and in the values of the Kingdom, so that when we gather, there is life and a sense of awe. Our job is to equip believers to do the work of the ministry by living out the values of the Kingdom. We are to be infected with Kingdom principles in such a way that we reproduce the Kingdom everywhere we go.

When I (Larry) got right with God at the age of 18, my life was turned upside down. It was a bit like Mr. Hyde returning to his identity as Dr. Jekyll. One day I was cursing a blue streak, and the next day I was speaking kindly to everyone. I no longer had any desire to "live in the fast lane," looking for a cheap thrill. I just wanted more of Jesus. I had begun to devour the Bible, one book at a time. I wrote out a verse of Scripture on a 3x5 card every day and placed it on my sun visor so I could memorize it. Little did I know that these hundreds of memorized verses of Scripture would come in so handy in years to come.

I got rid of everything that would hinder my love relationship with Jesus Christ. I just wanted to be with Him. I even stopped reading the daily comics for a season. That sounds crazy now, but I just did not want to waste my time. People around me were going to hell. I wanted to tell people about Jesus and help them grow in Christ. And I wanted someone to help me grow as a new believer in Christ as well.

But few people seemed to think like this. It was a rude awakening for me. Many Christians seemed content just to go to church each week, and they appeared to care little about those around them who needed Jesus in their lives. Then I really got ruined when I began to read the book of Acts. It seemed like everywhere Paul went, there was either revival or a riot; but everywhere I went, I only saw more religious tradition.

I began to attend a youth group Bible study with my girlfriend, LaVerne. The Bible study met in various people's homes and was sponsored by the Mennonite church where LaVerne's dad served as the pastor. This kind of scared me, since no one in my family had ever been a pastor. My family's ancestors were church attendees, but most seemed to be pretty nominal about their faith. So attending a Bible study was new to me.

The saving grace for me was that the youth of this church really wanted to study the Bible and experience true Christianity—where people really love Jesus, love the Church and love the lost. The more we studied the Bible together, the more we wanted to experience the book of Acts for ourselves. We saw that in the book of Acts people came to faith in Christ every day, and they met in community in their homes and loved one another, and everyone seemed to be serving and discipling others.

There should be no 20/80 rule in the Church. Everybody—not just 20 percent of the people—should be in 100 percent and discipling those coming behind them to be involved 100 percent as well. The North American Church has gotten comfortable with relegating evangelism and discipleship to a few staff members, paying them to do the work we have all been called to. Full-time paid ministers are not the only ones called by God to carry His values and live them out. Everyone in the Church needs to be engaged in the basic values of the Kingdom.

Christianity is not just a dream or a vision. It's a reality in which to engage. And the depths to which we engage determines the fruitfulness we'll see in our lives. When it comes right down to it, we must clarify our values around three biblical principles: loving God, loving each other, and loving the lost. We believe that as these values are simply lived out in community, we cannot help but bear fruit and see lives changed.

Value 1: Love God

People need to be daily before God, seeking Him in a devotional life that leads to a lifestyle of abiding in Jesus. No one has ever influenced the world around him or her for the glory of God without God's involvement.

We cannot live without God. We say that out of deep fear and trembling. If we do not spend time in prayer and the Word every day, we do not function properly. I (Jimmy) used to say jokingly, "If I miss a day, I get a little ornery. If I miss two days, I get mean. If I miss three days, I can commit just about any sin under the sun." While I used to say this just to prove a point, today I believe it to the core of my being. I don't have to eat. I don't have to sleep. I don't have to have a job or friends. But I have to have God.

Most of us do not feel we need God that much. If you are not compelled to be in God's presence by need, then be there by choice. By choice make decisions to try to learn in the journey. And as that journey continues, God will help you to recognize your need for Him. If we, as a Church, are not meeting with God, meditating on and digesting His truth, we will be weak and anemic, and that glorious Church we are called to be will never be seen.

As a college student, I was invited to lunch at Robert Ewing's house. Robert had been healed of stuttering as a teenager and called to an apostolic ministry. He had students over to his house and told stories of God's work around the world. The unique thing about Robert was that to be in his presence was like being in the presence of the Lord. He was a 60-year-old single man who had chosen to completely belong to God.

Sometimes I couldn't grasp Robert's deep teaching, but there was something about his intimacy with God that drew me to him. I asked him, "Robert, how do you love Jesus so much? How do you live such a pure life and carry the presence of the Lord so wonderfully?"

Robert replied, "First of all, Jimmy, you need to know that it is not me, but God working in me. For the last 40 years, I have started off my days by meditating on Scripture about the cross." He shared with me out of Isaiah 53, Hebrews 9 and 10, and Psalm 103. Robert told me, "I meditate on the cross every day, and I identify with it. I roll off my concerns and anxieties into the person of Christ, and then I go into my day and I walk with the Lord. At the end of the day, I come to the cross again, and I unburden the hurts and struggles of the day. I wake up in the cross and I go to sleep in the cross. That is how you live free in love. That is how you remain pure and holy before God."

That truth transformed my life. Christianity should not be wrapped up in religious exercises and principles, but in the person of Jesus Christ. I began to meditate daily on passages about God Almighty, the person of Jesus, and the Holy Spirit. It is still my habit today, years later, to live and sleep in the cross on a daily basis. That practice has allowed me to experience freedom, joy and grace through trials and struggles. More than anything, it has kept me centered as I live in a world that pulls me in a hundred different directions.

This must be our ultimate pursuit in life. Christ must be the One consuming us, and out of that we do His bidding for His glory. We have found that intimacy with God is the hinge on which every issue in life turns. If we are connecting wholeheartedly with God, then we are able to live in His presence and accomplish what He has created us to do. Without Him, we are truly nothing.

Robert described it this way: The person of Christ must always be first in our lives; the purposes of Christ should be the natural outflow of that devotion; the projects of Christ are the practical expression of His will. Person, then purpose, then projects. If those priorities ever get out of order, then we will miss the heart of God along the way.

So, to keep Jesus first in our lives, we have encouraged our people to be committed to seeking God in the Word, worshiping, and praying before they do anything else each morning. We believe that doing this first keeps us in love with Jesus—able to work from a place of great grace and fueled with the strength, energy, wisdom and counsel we need to continue on in all that God has for us to do.

When I (Larry) was a young believer in Christ, meeting with the Mennonite youth group for Bible study, I loved going to Kathryn's home with the other youth. Kathryn was an older Mennonite lady who really intrigued me. She was a single mom who lived alone with her adult daughter who had special needs. She never talked about it, but we all knew that her husband had left her years ago, immediately after their daughter was born with Down syndrome.

Kathryn was so in love with Jesus. You could literally sense the presence of God in her home. She loved spending time alone with the Lord each day and had learned to practice His presence. He had become her Bridegroom. She had an intimate relationship with Him. Kathryn was completely fulfilled in her relationship with Jesus. She had no lack in her life. When thousands of young people met in an open field in the 1970s in south-central Pennsylvania for the early "Jesus Gatherings" during the Jesus movement, Kathryn was right there in the midst of them—worshiping her Lord.

She had a deep impact on my life and on many of those in our youth Bible study group. She had learned to have an intimate walk with the Lord, and when you were in her presence, you felt like you were in the presence of Jesus Himself. God was teaching me through this godly woman that getting in His presence each morning is where it all begins.

A few years later, my wife and I helped to start a youth ministry to unreached teens in a community near our home in Pennsylvania. We called this ministry "Lost But Found." When troubled young people came to faith in Christ, we began to teach them the importance of spending time daily with God by praying and reading His Word and getting to know Him as a friend. The value of loving Jesus is where it all begins. We want to spend time with those we love.

And now, many years later, what is thrilling and exciting about this value is not just seeing our own people engaging with God and being transformed through spending time daily alone with Him. As we have gone to the nations of the world, we have passed this value on to those we have led to Christ and discipled. National leaders are now exhorting their own people to seek God first in the mornings and develop a love relationship with Him. When we gather with these leaders, it is so awesome to see them spend hours at the beginning of their day praying and in the Word. This simple truth has changed our lives, and it continues to change lives all over the world.

Value 2: Love Each Other

God has put His life within us so that we might give our lives away for others. Who is it that God has put in your life for you to show compassion towards: a neighbor, a friend, someone nearby? But you know it's not just a general compassion that changes the world. It's an intentional compassion that we call *discipleship*.

Larry and I often ask the question, "Who are you investing in?" Just as people have invested in us, we should invest in others so that God can reproduce life among us. While we are structured in small groups, outside of that people meet in twos and threes for discipleship. These discipleship relationships empower the small groups and the church. No one is left out or excused from this expectation. We ask everyone to invest in one, two or three people in such a way that they, too, are equipped to invest in others. One of our core values is that discipleship must happen, and it must reproduce.

Because this has been our focus from the beginning, we now have whole generations of disciple makers in our midst. Today, those groups of discipled people are serving as disciple-making communities around the world.

We believe that every Christian should be committed to discipleship so that the kingdom of God can invade his or her sphere of influence. Every politician needs somebody discipling him or her. If they are discipled rightly, then Kingdom values will be lived out in their offices. Every businessperson, health care professional, educator, parent, and so on, needs to be discipled. When the values of the Kingdom are imparted, the whole of society will be affected.

Years ago, Larry and I both began the simple process of investing in men's and women's lives with the expectation that they would do the same. Neither of us was trying to start a church movement; we just desired to obey the Bible and invest spiritually in others in order to make disciples. Since then, we have seen generation after generation of people who, by investing in one another's lives, are bearing fruit all over the world.

In the mid 1990s, a young man named Mark came to be a part of our training school (a nine-month intensive discipleship class based out of our local church and focused on restoration and missions) and began investing in Baylor College students. I invested in Mark's life, and he invited a number of guys into an intentional relationship of seeking God together. He started with four guys who took seriously the teachings of Jesus and began to reproduce the life of Jesus in others. One of those was a guy named Robert, and as Mark and I together began to invest in Robert, Robert began to invest in a guy named Jonathan. Jonathan began to invest in a guy named Jady. Jady gathered a group of athletes together and began to challenge them with the issues of sin in their lives. They started to get set free and began to abandon their lives radically to the Lord.

Out of those five steps of discipleship has come great fruit all over the world. Robert is our church plant leader in San Diego, California; Jonathan is our church plant leader in Chicago, Illinois; and Jady is our church plant leader in Seattle, Washington. One of the guys that he brought into his group, Chris, served with Jonathan on the church-planting team in Chicago before heading out to lead our church-planting work in India. And each of these guys has led many, many people to Jesus. Each of them is currently discipling and reproducing house church leaders in the countries and cities in which God has called them to serve. A couple of years ago, we did the math and realized that there were literally hundreds of disciples just from that initial group of men. As I had an opportunity and privilege to meet with Mark, he intentionally invested in a group of young people, and now hundreds, if not thousands, of people all over the world are being affected.

With so many of the people we've had the privilege of discipling now serving around the world, we now have the joy of meeting the men and women in whom they are investing—people who are leaders in their respective countries. Truly faithful discipleship in your own location will and does touch the nations of the earth.

Who are you investing in? Who are the people God has put right before you that with some intentional, loving, caring investment could end up changing the world around them? We never know the full impact of our intentional love and care for those around us. One thing we know for sure is that God is committed to multiplying our lives above and beyond what we could ask or think. Are you multiplying your life today?

The discipleship process really does work. God can take one life and multiply it to the unreached of the earth again and again. During the past two months, I (Larry) traveled thousands of miles to three different continents outside of the United States to minister to church leaders, and in every place I visited, I was privileged to minister to church leaders who had been discipled by our spiritual sons and daughters or spiritual grandsons and granddaughters.

In Africa, there are many who call me their spiritual "grandfather." I am deeply honored and so grateful to the Lord for this divine opportunity. In reality, most of these African leaders are my spiritual great-great-grandsons and -granddaughters. And this all started when I made a conscious decision, nearly 30 years ago when I was a chicken farmer in Pennsylvania, to make disciples. One of the men God called me to pour my life into was Ibrahim, a Kenyan who was a university student in the United States. Ibrahim then moved back to Kenya to serve as a journalist and, eventually, to plant a new church in Nairobi with neighbors he and his wife, Diane, had led to Christ.

Ibrahim and Diane planted this first DOVE church in Nairobi, Kenya, in 1989. "DOVE" is an acronym for "Declaring Our Victory Emmanuel," and it began in 1980 when LaVerne and I and a team of young leaders started a new church in Pennsylvania. By the grace of God, within 10 years this new church grew into a congregation of more than 2,000 people involved in discipleship relationships, with a vision to start churches throughout the world. The church that Ibrahim and Diane planted was the first seed of a church-planting multiplication process that has now grown exponentially throughout East Africa and beyond. Ibrahim and those he mentored poured their lives into others who have planted churches in several African nations and now in India as well.

One of the men whom Ibrahim poured his life into was a student from Uganda named Ephraim. Ibrahim was a teacher at DayStar University when he met Ephraim and became a spiritual father to him. Ephraim joined the DOVE church in Nairobi, and when it came time for him to move back home to Kampala, Uganda, he and his wife, Jova, started a church made up of new believers in the Kampala area. Today, Ephraim is a discipler of leaders of leaders, and those he has influenced have started and currently lead more than 60 congregations all over the nation. Ephraim continues to call Ibrahim his "spiritual father"—and he calls me his "spiritual grandfather"! That makes me sound pretty old, but it doesn't matter. I have experienced such joy in watching the Lord, by His grace, multiply disciples throughout the world through God-given healthy relationships.

Here's the story of just one of the church planters Ephraim discipled and trained. Paul was brought up in witchcraft. When he heard the good news that Jesus could set him free, he embraced the message of salvation wholeheartedly. After being discipled by Ephraim, Paul felt God's call to church planting and reaching those who desperately needed Jesus.

His first church started with 10 people meeting in an abandoned building. The former owner had left it vacant because a witch doctor told him that he had to abandon it to the devil because family members were falling sick and some had died.

The church grew and thrived, and Paul and his wife turned over leadership of the congregation to another couple and moved to a different village and into another house with a similar story of being inhabited by demons. Paul spiritually cleaned the house and used the abandoned sofas and other chairs for the church meetings. The non-believers in the community gave his family a few days to live in this demon-infested house. Days became weeks, and months became years, and Paul and his family and church have not died! In fact, Paul soon became famous for defying demons and occupying the haunted houses. He often prayed for the demon-possessed to be set free.

One example is that of a five-year-old boy named Charles. His father brought him to a church meeting for prayer because he was troubled by his young child's actions. The boy would neither eat nor drink, and he was growing quite thin. The father also said that his son enjoyed spending most of his time seated at his late grandfather's grave.

It seems that his late grandfather had chosen Charles to be the heir for his witchcraft powers. Words had been spoken to this boy by his grandfather. Charles's dad was saved and did not want his son to inherit the dead man's powers of witchcraft.

Believers in Jesus from the local church laid their hands on the boy and commanded the demonic powers that were pronounced by his grandfather on his body and life to leave him in the name of Jesus of Nazareth. Charles was delivered from the demonic powers that possessed him and is presently involved in the church.

In Paul's zeal to see people delivered and healed, he has traveled to many parts of eastern Uganda. Many have received Christ as their Lord and Savior through his ministry. He is currently overseeing more than 15 congregations in eastern Uganda, and he passionately loves and serves his Christ as he reproduces disciples.

I am always encouraged when I see Paul while visiting East Africa to serve both Ibrahim and Ephraim by ministering at conferences to help them train and release more leaders. Paul simply exudes the Spirit of Jesus and walks in a deep humility and great power. God continues to multiply His Kingdom through Paul and those he has led to Christ, who are now discipling others for continual Kingdom expansion. Paul is only one of many stories I could tell of those whom Ephraim has discipled and trained who are now "leaders of leaders."

The individuals I serve with on our international leadership team have been my friends for more than 25 years, as we have been in relationship together, learning how to live out biblical community. Biblical community is community with a purpose, not just community for community's sake.

When discipleship is at the core of your relationships, life-giving community happens. Community for community's sake is a dead-end street. In the emerging generation, there is a major interest in community, but we need to make sure there is a purpose driving us. As the people of God, we are knit at the hip and the heart because we are joined together for a purpose—not for our own purposes but for the purposes and values of the Kingdom for the glory of God.

Jesus said, "Go therefore and make disciples . . . teaching them to observe all that I commanded you . . ." (Matt. 28:19, *NASB*). We are driven by discipleship, and that is why we consistently evaluate and ask one another, "Who are you intentionally investing in, and how are they reproducing the Kingdom out of what you are giving them?"

Value 3: Love Those Who Do Not Yet Know Jesus

The gospel is the power of God for the salvation of everyone who believes (see Rom. 1:16). It is what sets people free. No matter how much good work we do, no matter how many different ideas we have about how to most effectively share the gospel, ultimately the gospel has power in and of itself to save. Our desire is to share the gospel in every way God makes possible to us.

In 1991, I (Jimmy), along with the training school students, found myself in the middle of an outpouring of God's Spirit in the country of Bulgaria. Daily we would go out, share the gospel, pray for the sick—and see God moving powerfully. After several days of early mornings and late nights spent serving others, our team was worn out and tired. As I released our team early one evening so they could get some rest, there were still more than 100 people lingering in the street waiting for us to minister.

Our young college student translator, who had been with us the whole time, tirelessly serving, began to tug on my shirt. "Mr. Jimmy, Mr. Jimmy, what are you doing?" I told her that I needed to let our people get some rest because they were so tired. She looked at me and, as tears began to roll down her cheeks, she asked, "Why are you in such a hurry when people are so hungry for Jesus?" At that moment I realized that the compassion of Jesus was greater than the compassion of my heart. People are the centerpiece of His heart, and it was worth staying and giving our lives. That night would be one of the most powerful incidences we would ever experience of God's power and grace being poured out on people.

That simple question—"Why are we in such a hurry when people are so hungry for Jesus?"—should ring in our ears day by day. Jesus looked on the multitudes with compassion because they were distressed and downcast like sheep without a shepherd, and He said, "Send more laborers." Did you know that every time we give a cup of cold water in the name of Jesus, it puts a smile on His face? Every time you spend a little extra time with a child, with a friend, or with someone who is hurting, it touches the heart of God.

When I came into a true living relationship with Christ, I knew I needed to learn to tell others about Him. This was not necessarily an easy thing for me to do at first, but the love of Christ within me began to compel me to share the gospel with others. I know that gospel tracts may not be for everyone, but this is how I got started. I made sure I never left home without them. I worked in construction for a season, and I kept tracts in my hardhat so that whenever I felt the Lord wanted me to give one to someone, I was ready.

For the many years I served as a senior pastor, we emphasized the three disciplines of prayer, making disciples and personal evangelism. And for years, seldom did a week go by when people were not coming to faith in Christ. We baptized these new believers in creeks, swimming pools and bathtubs, and we encouraged those who led them to Christ to be involved in baptizing these new converts. It felt like the book of Acts all over again. I am still thrilled when I regularly hear the stories of people from the DOVE family of churches throughout our nation and the world leading people to Christ in their communities. There is simply nothing like it!

Nora, who serves the Lord in a DOVE church in Bulgaria, is a young woman who received Jesus when a friend from the church challenged her about her relationship with the Lord. Since then, she has been discipled and is now committed to letting those who are living in the broken world around her know about the Jesus who has changed her life. Here is her story about God's process of training her to share her faith with others:

> One evening, I was talking with a friend and stated that I didn't know how to share with people about God. Well, I got that opportunity very quickly! On my walk home, I noticed a man approaching me. Before I knew it, he was just a few feet away. He shouted at me, hit me in the face, grabbed my arm, and snarled, "Give me your money."
>
> Without thinking, I stretched out my hand to him and said, "Jesus! God loves you!" Suddenly he froze and looked to the ground. His face was filled with guilt. Immediately words began to pour out of my mouth. I told him how much God loved him, and that nothing on this earth could compare to what the Lord could give him.
>
> He stared at me and asked, "Are you a believer?"
>
> I answered, "Yes, I believe in Jesus!" I shared with him about Jesus and His sacrifice on the cross. Our conversation continued for over 30 minutes. While we were talking, people began to pass by, and I could have run away. Though I was still scared, I felt the power of the Lord, and I was able to stay and keep sharing the good news.
>
> Finally I asked him if he wanted to repent and receive Jesus into his life, and he said, "Yes." During the prayer, he was crying and deeply touched. He apologized for what he had done and shook my hand.

I thought to myself, *Just an hour ago, I was complaining to my friend that I didn't know how to evangelize and lead someone to receive Jesus, and here I am doing it!*

I love our people because they share Christ everywhere they go. All over our city, on a daily basis, our people are sharing their testimonies and explaining simply and clearly how people can respond to the gospel message. One of our teachers, Amanda, tells this story from her classroom:

One week ago, school was so tough that I was ready to call it quits. Things were just too intense. I teach art at two schools, so I see roughly 500 children every two weeks. At one school in particular, things were really difficult. So on Tuesday my husband, Ed, and I went and prayed over my room.

On Wednesday, I was passing out coloring sheets to my kindergarten class, and I had two copies that were gray instead of white. I turned it into a good thing by saying, "Congratulations! You got one of the gray copies!" and one little boy said, "Thank You, Lord Jesus!"

I asked him to repeat himself, and he said the same thing. So then I asked him, "Who is Jesus?" and he said, "Jesus is God!"

I said, "That's right! What did Jesus do?"

Another little girl said, "He died on the cross."

So I asked, "Do you know why He died on the cross?" And the whole room fell silent. By this point the entire class of kindergarteners was paying attention. I told them the story about how Jesus was so powerful He calmed the sea, and how He healed people because He loved them. Then I said, "Raise your hand if you want to ask Jesus into your heart to be your Savior, forgive your sins, and be the boss of your life." Almost the entire class raised their hands. I led them in the salvation prayer. After I said, "Amen," the entire class began clapping and cheering! Thank You, Jesus!

Yeah! This thing works. Our people are out in the city handing out tracts, praying for people, and sharing the gospel. Some of our young mothers found a way to actively pursue loving those separated from God. They had grown tired of thinking they couldn't do anything for the Kingdom because they were at home all day with their small children, so they got together and prayed. Then they started going together to places like parks, where one mom could watch all the kids and the other moms could share the good news about Christ's purposes on earth. These women saw some people find hope for life and others join small groups. They put practical feet to their commitment to evangelism and found a way to make it happen. When we sow, we reap; when we do not sow, we do not reap.

We've heard people say that evangelism is not their calling. Our understanding of Scripture is that sharing the gospel is everyone's calling. This is an awesome calling because as we share Christ with others, we *will* see lives changed and transformed. We all get to be a part of God's grace as it comes to those headed in the wrong direction and rescues them from missing the mark and rejecting God. The following story is a great example of one of the moms in our midst, Beth, who did some "outside of the box" evangelism:

While living in Hewitt, the Lord put on my heart to minister to the folks who pick up our trash and recyclables by giving them cold sodas or water each week. He brought to mind the passage that says if we do these things "unto the least, we do it unto Him" (see Matt. 25:35-40).

As a homeschooling mother of four, I sometimes find it a bit of a challenge to get out to share the truth and love of Jesus with others. So, I decided to be more proactive with those who came to our house. The kids totally got into it, too! Each week we would set out the drinks and then often greet the folks as they came to our house. We slowly developed a relationship with Ladi, the UPS driver who delivered packages in our neighborhood. We also developed a friendship with the man who drove the recycling truck. He is a believer, and we were able to pray with and for him on numerous occasions. Once, when the kids laid hands on him to pray for him he was brought to tears!

Even though Ladi did not stop at our house every day, we could hear his truck and would take drinks outside when he drove by and/or stopped at a nearby house for a delivery. After a couple of drinks (ha, you know what I mean!), I asked him if he went to church. He said that his wife went to church, but that he preferred to watch football. I began to tell him about Antioch Church—how you can really experience the presence of God, how the messages are so relevant, how awesome the worship is, how genuine the people are, how life-changing Life-groups are, etc. For a long time, Ladi had no "realized need" for God. We continued to give him sodas.

Over time, God began working in Ladi's life through circumstances in his family. Ladi and his wife divorced. Ladi was at an all-time low. As a matter of fact, he drove by our house the day his divorce became final. I told him that God would help him through, and the kids and I prayed with and for him and invited him to church again.

After a year or more of relationship, Ladi came to Antioch. He was so touched by God; he said that he felt like the pastor was talking directly to him. A couple of months later, he came to our Lifegroup, where again he experienced the life and love of Jesus from everyone.

God has been doing incredible things in Ladi's life. God is in the process of reconciling Ladi's marriage. Ladi got baptized a couple of months ago. Now his former wife is coming to Antioch, and their entire family is coming to our Lifegroup. People at UPS are noticing a difference in Ladi's life, and he is giving all the glory to God. It's so obvious that Ladi is indeed a changed man. My husband, Matt, is pursuing a mentoring/discipling relationship with him. Matt and I have been out on double dates with him and his former wife.

Since then, we've moved into town and are now working on Chuck, our new UPS driver!

As a side note: As soon as I had the opportunity, I introduced the recycling worker and Ladi to my husband, and I made reference to my husband often in conversation. I wanted to stay aboveboard with them and to show them that it's all about Jesus!

Beth signs this testimony: "Reaching Waco one soda at a time!"

One Sunday, at the end of church, a single mom came up to me (Jimmy) with her little boy in her arms. She told me that she worked with a woman from church named Susan. They had become friends over time, and Susan had encouraged her and prayed for her consistently. While this young woman had no interest in the things of God, she found great comfort in the face of life's struggles and challenges as Susan counseled, encouraged and helped her.

Eventually, after many invitations, she went with Susan to a small group. Her own admission to me was that it was a little weird being there, but because of her friendship with Susan, she continued to go for several weeks. More and more, she found herself wanting to know God, which eventually led to her coming to Sunday services.

She told me, "I was actually really scared to come here, and I sat in the very back. After a couple of weeks, as I heard you sharing, I was deeply drawn in. I got a CD of one of the messages and listened to it while I was driving to work a few weeks ago. You talked about God's love for us and our need to know Him. I found myself crying uncontrollably, and I pulled off to the side of the road and gave my heart and life to Jesus. The last few weeks have been wonderful and life-changing as I have found people to walk with and to love me."

This young woman went on, "The reason I told you that story is that I wanted to introduce you to my little son, Ryan. I wanted to let you know that because of your people and this message of the gospel, his destiny will be different. He also will be a man of God."

Right there, I could have gone to heaven and been happy. The process works. A community of people loved and cared for a young woman, and the destiny of generations has been changed.

Love God. Love each other. Love the lost. Do you think these values aren't worth living out? Do you think it isn't worth laying it all down so that you can see lives changed? This is worth giving your life for. There is no cost too great when the return is for all to hear and know the truth—for all to see Jesus glorified. If you love Jesus and are obsessed with Him—if you love the Church and have biblical conviction—then what else can you do but give your all?

Because humans tend to make following God too complicated, God summed His commandments up into two very simple sentences: " 'You must love the Lord your God with all your heart, all your soul, all your strength, and all your mind.' And, 'Love your neighbor as yourself' " (Luke 10:27).

As a believer, your prayer must be that you will never lose these simple responses to God. As a result, you will be known for reproducing these Kingdom values of "loving God, loving each other, and loving those who do not yet know Jesus" in the uttermost parts of the earth. That is your destiny, and that must be the passion of every Jesus-follower.

LOVING
JESUS

Loving Jesus with a Passion

Telling our stories of learning to be passionate about Jesus

The summer that God touched my (Jimmy's) life so significantly as I read the simple words of Jesus and attempted to do them would leave me never the same. However, I soon found out that it wasn't just about me being changed; God also wanted to bring about transformation in and through a group of people. When I returned to college that fall, I discovered several other friends had encountered God in a similar way. My friends and I decided to gather in our apartment one evening to share stories of what God was doing. Other friends came along just to be with us, and as they heard the stories of God moving in our hearts, one after another they began to confess their sin.

As they shared, we just naturally gathered around them, laid hands on them, and prayed. As far as I knew, none of us had heard of the laying on of hands, but the presence of God was so real that the Holy Spirit was taking over and teaching us. Our time together that night began at 7:00 and went well past midnight as many of us experienced God, not just in a personal way, but now also as a community. That experience marked us for the rest of our college years, and for many of us the rest of our lives, as we realized that the Holy Spirit will move not just in a person but in a people in order to heal and restore lives.

For the first time in my life, I understood the reality of Luke's statement that "everyone kept feeling a sense of awe" (Acts 2:43, *NASB*). There was something about those gatherings that was powerful. Though some would ridicule us, others were drawn and changed by the presence of the Lord.

One day after class, my roommate and I were hanging out at our apartment, and we decided to pray together. As we were on our knees, seeking the Lord, I told him that I was seeing a picture in my mind. He said he was seeing one, too. I explained that I saw a road with Jesus walking down the middle. There were people in the ditches on both the right and left sides. It seemed to me that we were to walk down the middle with Jesus. My roommate told me he was seeing the same thing.

As we prayed and talked about this, we realized that this picture had to do with a common debate in the Church at that time regarding conservative versus charismatic theology. We felt like Jesus was telling us that people had fallen to the right and to the left, but if we would just follow Him, we would always be on the right path. This vision has marked both of our walks with the Lord ever since. We learned that we were never to get caught up in one side or the other, but simply to follow Jesus.

After college, my plans were to go to seminary so that I could go into full-time pastoral ministry. The morning I was walking to the mailbox to send my completed application to Fuller Theological Seminary, the Lord intercepted me so strongly that I doubled over in the driveway. I was not supposed to go to seminary.

Though I was confused, I knew God was speaking to me, so I walked back into the house and threw the application away. "What do You have for me, Lord?" I asked. He didn't answer me right away.

As I sat down to study for a finance test though, He spoke to me and said, "I want you to go into business."

"But, God, I gave all that up," I protested. "When You said, 'Follow Me,' I gave up my pursuit of business and chose to follow You."

Immediately I heard Him say, "Trust Me, and I'll lead you the right way."

At that time, my wife, Laura, and I were engaged, and we had already committed to say yes to Jesus no matter what, so I began looking for business opportunities. One opened up in Houston—I got a job working for a medical supply company. After graduation, I packed up and moved to Houston, while Laura stayed in Waco to finish school.

For me, there was only one goal for my time in Houston: learn to love God more than ever by learning to abide in Him. Every morning, I read and meditated on John 15:1-15. I would think and pray through these verses and do everything I could to apply them to my life. Before I went to work, I focused on the words of John 15:5: "I am the vine, you are the branches; he who abides in Me and I in him, he bears much fruit, for apart from Me you can do nothing" (*NASB*). The phrase that repeated over and over in my mind through each day was "apart from You, I can do nothing."

Out of that simple abiding relationship, I saw God move powerfully while I worked in business. By listening and talking to people, I had opportunities to share Christ, see people healed, and see lives redirected. I found God's presence so near that it seemed, moment by moment, that I tangibly knew He was with me. Some of my fondest memories of walking intimately with the Lord are from those days. No one had talked to me about how to be a Christian businessman; it just happened because I wanted to follow Jesus. I learned that wherever God puts me vocationally, the answer to bearing fruit in that place is simply to listen and obey God.

One day, I overslept and had to rush out the door without the chance to meditate on John 15. Though I tried to quote Scripture to myself throughout the day, it just seemed like I wasn't in sync with the Lord. That evening, I went to a friend's church where they opened up the altar at the end of the service so people could come forward and pray. I got on my knees and started to sob uncontrollably. I thought, *God, what is happening?* I found these words coming out of my mouth: "I miss You! I miss You! I miss You!" You see, I had grown so accustomed to abiding and living in His presence, that when I didn't connect with Him first thing in the morning, I missed Him as the day went on.

That summer, I got so addicted to Jesus—to abiding in Him—that I found it was too difficult to live life apart from Him. For me, apart from Him, I can truly do nothing.

Abiding in Him

When I (Larry) turned the ripe old age of 20, I asked my girlfriend, LaVerne, to marry me, and we decided to take the first year of our new life together to serve on the mission field. My plan was to return to Pennsylvania, continue working on the family farm with my father, and eventually take over the family business. I had no plan to become a full-time paid pastor; in fact, I did not want to be a pastor at all. I loved Jesus, but I just did not want to become a pastor. I had learned early on as a believer in Christ that every believer is a minister regardless of occupation, and I wanted to be known simply as a Christian, not a pastor. I felt like becoming a pastor would place me in a box and make me un-relatable to the average Joe. I just wanted to live life, serve Jesus, tell others about Him, and then help new believers grow spiritually.

LaVerne and I got married in October 1971 at the ages of 19 and 20, respectively, and three weeks later we arrived on John's Island, South Carolina, to lead a stateside mission base for the Mennonite Church. We served with a missionary team that tore down houses in Charleston, took the nails out of the lumber, and then reused this wood to build houses for the families who were poor on the adjacent islands. At every opportunity, we shared our faith in Christ with our new friends on John's Island and the nearby islands.

But it was here that I really learned the importance of spending time with God each morning and growing in my love relationship with Him. It was here that I also learned to stay attached to Jesus, the Vine. I had heard that Hudson Taylor, the famous missionary, one day found he was very depressed, and as he walked in the forest he heard God say to him that he should look at a tree. "What do you see?" the Lord asked him.

"I see a tree and I see branches," he said.

And then God asked him, "What are the branches doing?"

"Just staying attached to the tree," said Hudson.

And then God replied, "And that is all I am asking you to do, Hudson. Stop trying so hard. Just stay attached to the vine." Obviously, God was referring to the words of Jesus in John 15:5 when He said, "Yes, I am the vine; you are the branches. Those who remain in me, and I in them, will produce much fruit. For apart from me you can do nothing."

Regardless of what I was experiencing on the island, I referred back, again and again, to this truth of staying attached to

Jesus. Without Him, I could do absolutely nothing. This was not just a Scripture verse to me; it was a deep reality. I needed Jesus desperately.

I became a student of His Word on this island, and I walked with God in the woods behind our home each day and listened for Him to speak to me. I just stayed attached to the Vine. He gave me divine wisdom to give leadership to the mission on many occasions. This mission location had a history of struggles among missionaries, and our mission overseer was amazed that things seemed to go so well for us. We were keenly aware that we were simply experiencing the grace of God as we daily learned to listen to Him.

I was desperate to hear His voice each day—so that I could give effective leadership to our team, and so I could talk to people in our community about Jesus. God gave us a deep love for these precious people. We were in the School of the Holy Spirit, being prepared for our future of taking the love of Jesus to many different cultures of the world.

They Loved Jesus with All Their Hearts

During a mission trip to Papua New Guinea as a college student, I (Jimmy) caught a vision for the Kingdom and would never look at life the same way again. One day, our team drove through the countryside as far as the Land Cruiser would take us, and then we hiked up the side of a mountain. As we entered the village, it seemed that the love of God overwhelmed us. The people ran toward us and embraced us as if we'd known one another for a lifetime. Although I didn't know the language, somehow the language of God communicated for us. After sharing a meal together, the villagers asked me to preach.

At that point in my life, I only knew a couple of Scripture passages by memory—one of which I had learned the night before: "For God has not given us a spirit of fear, but of power and of love and of a sound mind" (2 Tim. 1:7, *NKJV*). Since that verse was so fresh on my mind, I thought it was a good place to start preaching.

We sang a few songs in the local language, Tok Pisin, and then through two translators, I preached. As I spoke, I began to cry. Then those listening began to cry. The presence of God filled the meeting place, and we worshiped together for the next few hours. Whenever I opened my eyes and looked around, it seemed to me that the walls were shaking. I was reminded of Acts 4, where it says, "the place where they had gathered together was shaken, and they were all filled with the Holy Spirit and began to speak the word of God with boldness" (Acts 4:31, *NASB*).

The book of Acts came alive that day. No matter what the debates were back home about expressions of worship and spiritual gifts, I had experienced reality—the reality of Christ among a humble people who loved Him with all of their hearts. These people were contriving absolutely nothing. They had simply met a Savior and were living out the reality of the Kingdom by worshiping Him with all of their hearts. This picture still sticks in my mind as I yearn and hunger for the same thing to happen in communities here in our own nation.

A Deep Love for Jesus Causes Us to Look Outward

When I (Larry) came fully to Jesus as an 18-year-old, God began to change me immediately. I started reading the Bible, and the words leapt off the page. Before, I could hardly read a verse without experiencing extreme boredom, but now a deep love for Jesus developed. To be a Christian means to imitate Christ, and I wanted to do what Jesus did: love others and invest in those around me.

When we returned to Pennsylvania from our stateside mission stint in 1972, our nation was still coming out of the tumultuous 1960s with rapid changes tearing at the fabric of society, including the sexual revolution, Vietnam War, women's liberation and abortion rights. Young people had dabbled in the occult and the drug culture seeking answers for life but were disillusioned. They were now seeking God in great numbers, and this influx of young people turning to Jesus became known as the Jesus Movement. It was a time of a nationwide revival in the United States, and the Church was challenged in these uncertain times because young people started to question everything about traditional Church.

Interest in the Rapture theory grew during this time due to the books of Hal Lindsey. In his book *The Late Great Planet Earth*, Lindsey predicted an imminent Rapture based on global conditions at the time. Then a film called *A Thief in the Night* presented the possible events surrounding the Rapture in a startling way, creating widespread public interest in the end-time theory.

These events served as a wake-up call. Complacent Christian young people were jolted from their apathy, as they were exhorted to get right with God because the end could be very near. Many of these same Christian young people developed a genuine burden for their world. I was one of those young people. LaVerne and I, along with a group of Christian friends, developed a burden for the youth in our community in northern Lancaster County, Pennsylvania. We had helped start a youth ministry to unchurched teens in the area just before we were married and entered the mission field. So, when we returned a year later to serve with my father on the family farm, we joined this team that had set out to initiate creative and culturally effective ways to reach these kids with the love of Jesus. We sincerely desired to love the youth as Jesus does, with actions as well as words. We wanted to go out to where the people were, like Jesus did. Jesus went to where the people that needed help tended to be. He worked to create an environment that was conducive to making people feel comfortable so they would better be able to receive what He had to say. We, too, wanted to create a place that felt natural to the kids so we could connect with them.

We started to go regularly into a local low-income community and play baseball with the youth in a vacant lot. Every week, rain or shine, we showed up to meet any kids that came. And they came. Not just teenagers, but younger kids who craved love and attention. We began to see the kids through Christ's eyes. We saw the pain that many of them carried. We spent many late nights gathering as a staff to pray fervently for the kids and their families and their many needs.

We knew we were in for the long haul, so we set up a nonprofit organization called "Lost But Found" and greatly expanded our ministry to the youth in that community. One of the homeowners in the community also owned a small vacant house. He offered it to us to use as a community center and coffee house where kids could hang out. We filled it with cast-off couches and chairs, a pool table, and other table games. Realizing the need for more structured activities for the young people who started to hang out at the house, we formed a variety of clubs for different age groups and interests of the kids. Before long, we also purchased a mobile home in the community and used it as the base for our many Bible and sports clubs, as well as other activities held almost every night of the week.

It was hard work and a huge commitment of our time. At times the kids seemed unappreciative and made fun of our efforts, but they continued to come and hang out, and we knew we were on the right track. We had a sense of expectancy that if we were faithful in sharing the gospel, then spiritual growth would happen, one decision at a time.

Our friendships with the kids deepened. Through friendship evangelism, we consistently shared the good news that Jesus Christ is available to change the life of anyone who decides to accept Him. We saw dozens of young people come to know Jesus as their Lord as we further expanded our ministry into several neighboring communities.

I was asked by our team to start a weekly Bible study for the youth who were new believers in Christ, so we could nurture these young Christians—teaching simple truths from Scripture and encouraging the kids to love Jesus with all their hearts. In this informal setting, kids started to experience church for the first time and get a taste of what loving Jesus and others was all about. Our outreach strategy was reaching a whole segment of the community who did not typically attend church and indeed often felt uncomfortable in more traditional church settings. During this time in my life, I realized just how important it is to stick to the basics of Christianity. New believers respond to Jesus with a simple faith, believing deep down that He is alive and that He will help them through their personal brokenness. It's that simple and that profound.

Sometimes we drift away from simply trusting Jesus because it's easier to follow a set of directions. We can find ourselves relating to God by following a set list of things to do:

verses to practice, Bible passages to read, a certain number of minutes to pray. However, Jesus is not a biblical principle to apply. We must learn to know Him and trust Him as Savior, Lord and friend. We do this by getting to know Him through the Scriptures, and then by the personal experiences of meeting with Him, trusting Him, and longing for more. We long for more than knowledge about Jesus; we long for Jesus Himself.

When we have a dynamic, life-changing relationship with Jesus Christ, we're not just proclaiming a written word; we're proclaiming the Living Word. "We proclaim to you the one who existed from the beginning, whom we have heard and seen. We saw him with our own eyes and touched him with our own hands. He is the Word of life" (1 John 1:1).

Danail, a young pastor in his twenties from one of the DOVE churches in Bulgaria, has a passion to spread the message of God's reality in the university where he studies music. He is a brilliant musician and a lover of Jesus. Through the years he has taken advantage of every opportunity to be a living testimony and proclaim the Living Word.

While working on a project with a singer, Danail shared the gospel with her several times and introduced her to people from the church. After a few weeks they met again online and, prompted by God's Spirit, Danail told this young woman that it was time for her to say "yes" to God. That evening she gave her life to Christ—online! Now she is being discipled by her pastor's daughter and is growing rapidly in the Lord.

Another singer from the class Danail teaches saw his profile on MySpace and discovered he was a Christian. The next day, she found him at school and said she's been looking for people whom she can talk to about God. Danail introduced her to DOVE church members, and they began to disciple her.

This young woman worked in a disco, and although the church members were tempted to tell her this was not a good place for a Christian to work, instead they just prayed. A few days later, the singer called the pastor's daughter and said she needed to meet her, urgently. They met in a coffee shop, and the girl started to cry. She said, "There is something holy in you, and I can't stay in your presence." She realized she had to quit her work in the disco, and she immediately called her boss. When she did, she said she felt as if she had been delivered of something and set free. Now this girl is on fire for God. She wants to know Him more and live for Him. She can't get enough of Jesus, and she shares His love with nearly everyone she meets.

As Christians—Christ-followers—we have met with Christ, we love Him in response to His love for us, and we need to be giving Him and His love away! Those are the values of the Kingdom. People who live out these values in the context of community change cities, families and nations. "Value Carriers"—that's what we want to be ! We really don't need to be big, and we don't need to be famous, but we do need Jesus. We need His love desperately. And each of us needs to be involved with a community of people who love Him with all of their hearts.

4

How Do You Say the Name of Jesus?

**Why we must experience a return to
just loving Jesus with a passion and developing
an intimate personal daily prayer life**

I (Jimmy) turned on the radio several years ago, and Heather
Mercer and Dayna Curry were the guests on James Dobson's
radio program. Heather and Dayna are two young women from
our church who were imprisoned in Afghanistan by the Taliban
for 104 days in 2001, because they were telling their Afghan
friends about Jesus. Dr. Dobson invited Heather and Dayna to
share their story with his radio audience.

On the air, as they spoke about what it was like to be in jail,
they told a story about hearing a man being beaten in the prison
cell next to theirs. Not knowing how else to respond to this
heinous act, they sat in their own cells and began singing the
song by Martin Smith, "There Is a Light." James Dobson was so
touched by this particular story that he asked them to sing the
song live on the radio.

Dr. Dobson cried as they sang, and when they were finished,
he asked them a very telling question: "Are you aware that when
you say the word *Jesus*, the name *Jesus*, you say it in a different

way than many other people do? You say it in a way that shows deep, deep love and appreciation and compassion and respect. Are you aware of that? It shows through not just in the way you say Jesus' name but in what you've done with your lives."

After Dr. Dobson's remark, I turned off the radio and prayed aloud, "Thank You, Jesus! I know a thousand more just like them." I know them, because they are in our church. These believers know Jesus, not by sight, not by someone else's description, but through a personal encounter day by day. They cultivate a lifestyle of seeking the face of God and living out the simple values of the Kingdom so that people see Jesus even in their most difficult trials.

Over the next months, as our church received worldwide media attention because of the girls who were imprisoned in Afghanistan, we went from being an unknown church to becoming a sought-after interview. As we met with so many people in the press during those months, we took the opportunity to minister to them. I remember one particular group, from one of the largest news agencies in the world, who visited our church service. After filming that Sunday, tears filled the reporter's eyes as he asked me, "What was that presence? I've seen a lot of religious services, but there was something different here. What was it?"

"That's Jesus," I responded, "the real Jesus—the One who loves you and cares for you and died for you."

There's Something About His Name

There's something about Jesus that is compelling. Like this news reporter, when people who don't know Him catch a glimpse of His presence, they find it hard to define. The presence of Jesus—that "something different" that manifests in the lives of those who have a relationship with Him, cannot go unnoticed.

Too often, people have experienced a form of religion and consequently consider Jesus to be little more than a religious figure. They may have attended church, prayed, obeyed the rules, and followed the traditions, but if they are not following Jesus, it is just dead religion that denies the work of Christ and the mercy and grace of God in their lives. Unless they know that Jesus demonstrated His deep love when He laid down His life for them, they are not following Jesus.

What we believe is of critical importance. The Bible says, "There is a way that seems right to a man, but in the end it leads to death" (Prov. 16:25, *NIV*). Today, as in biblical times, there are good, decent people who are deeply sincere about the spiritual road they are on—they are sure it's the right way— but that won't change the fact that it will end in death. Sincerity simply is not enough. Sincere people thought Goodyear was foolish for spending 11 years working on vulcanizing rubber, but today millions of people ride on Goodyear tires. Those who jeered were sincere, but sincerely wrong. Sincere people called Westinghouse a fool for daring to think he could stop a railroad train with wind. But today, Westinghouse air brakes are used all over the world.

Some years back, I (Larry) took my son to a restaurant in our hometown, and after enjoying a sandwich, I went to the restroom to wash my hands. Something felt a bit strange, but I was in a hurry and did not think much about it. When I opened the door of the restroom to return to the restaurant area, Josh was waiting for me just outside the door. His eyes were filled with horror. "Dad, you were in the women's restroom!" he exclaimed. I wheeled around to look at the sign, and he was right. I had mistakenly used the women's facilities! Thankfully, no one else had entered the restroom while I was there. You see, I was sincere, but sincerely wrong.

It really does matter what we believe, regardless of how sincere we are (see Acts 17:22-31). Jesus Christ is central to the gospel. There are other religions, other teachers and other prophets. But there is only one Jesus who claims to have died for our sins and paid the price to redeem us. Any hope of getting to know God is realized by putting trust in Jesus and having a dynamic and living personal relationship with Him.

The awesome truth is that Jesus Christ paid for all our sins on the cross—and has given us direct access to God! Jesus loves us for who we are, and before we ever came to Christ, He laid down His life for us. This is the central message we must preach and proclaim today.

We must know Him through a personal encounter day by day. We must cultivate a lifestyle of seeking the face of God so that people see Jesus in us. The future of the Church depends on people engaging Jesus and on the life of God being made manifest in their lives as they live out the simple values of the Kingdom. This involves having an intimate daily prayer life. Our spiritual foundations must be built on prayer.

A Foundation of Prayer

During different periods of our lives together at Antioch Community Church, I and the other leaders were burdened to lead the church in intense prayer. One time, we hosted several 3-day, 24-hour prayer and fasting times at the church, crying out for a move of the Holy Spirit. Camping out in the sanctuary and using sleeping bags for periods of rest, we believed and asked God for a breakthrough.

After several sessions like this, I (Jimmy) was discouraged that nothing seemed to be happening. I went to one of my mentors and asked him what we were doing wrong. I'll never forget Robert's wise words: "Many people want to see God move, but God always raises up intercessors first. When the move of God begins, everyone will be on the bandwagon, but you and God will know that you were a part of starting it."

Those days of learning how to pray laid the foundation for a lifestyle and culture of prayer in our community. We realized that no one has ever advanced God's kingdom in the world without becoming a person of intense, persevering prayer. The principles we learned during that year carry on, years later. I believe that it is our consistency in going before God personally and corporately that has not only sustained us but transforms us day by day.

God has designed prayer in such a way that when we cry out to Him, we are able to encounter Him in deep and powerful ways and are drawn into the relationship that we always longed for. Out of this intimacy, we are then able to see Him work. I love that, because when He works, we can't take any credit. Prayer is geared for us to partner in relationship with God, but for Him to get all of the glory.

Sometimes prayer can feel weak or unheard, but for those who persevere, there is always fruit. We are so thankful that He has consistently called us to pray, because now we can honestly look back and say that He alone has done it all. After experiencing His presence and power day after day, year after year through prayer, we press on, expecting and anticipating Him to continue to move in our midst.

Developing a Personal Prayer Life

Everyone wants to experience a satisfying prayer life, but it takes perseverance to consistently have that "Sweet Hour of Prayer." Most Christians know what it's like to be convicted and determined to pray more. We diligently set aside 15 or 30 minutes, or maybe an hour, each day to pray. The first few minutes are great as we thank Him for who He is, and for His love toward us, and for watching out for our family, and for giving us the strength to work, and for health and friends. Then, about 15 minutes later, we shake ourselves out of the day-dreaming daze we are in, realizing we have been planning the rest of our day, thinking about what to say to our boss about the project we're working on, and worrying about the bills coming due. We gulp and ask God to forgive us for wandering off, only to find ourselves repeating the same process all over again after a few more minutes.

I (Larry) have gone through various seasons in prayer during my walk with the Lord. During many seasons, I have experienced a deep intimacy with my heavenly Father. However, during other seasons, my prayer life has been a struggle. Something was missing. Then, some years ago, during a time when my personal prayer life felt a bit dry, I received a major wake-up call from the Lord.

I had gone to Uzbekistan, where persecution of Christians occurs in the forms of fines, loss of jobs, interrogation and imprisonment, to meet with leaders of the underground Church. More often than not, when I find myself in these settings, I feel that those I meet have much more to teach me than I can teach them, but they are typically very eager to receive biblical instruction and training.

On this particular occasion, after our team of three Christian leaders had taught from the Scriptures, our hosts asked us questions. One question penetrated to my core. "Tell us about your personal prayer life," one of the Uzbek Christian leaders asked. "How much time do you spend alone with God each day?" I was suddenly uncomfortable and convicted by the Lord. I had recently become very busy, and I was not spending as much time each day with Jesus as I knew I needed. I deferred the question to one of the other team members to avoid further embarrassment. I knew immediately I had been "weighed in the scales and found wanting." I left Uzbekistan with a deep conviction that I must learn again how to pray.

I fervently believed in prayer, and I had enjoyed many seasons of intimate times of prayer with my Lord. I taught on prayer, I went to all-night prayer meetings, I prayed daily, and I knew the importance of prayer in a Christian's life. I had seen countless answers to prayer in my life and in the lives of others around the world. But during this season of my life, prayer was difficult for me.

Prayer Brings Revival

When I visit many of the nations and cities of the world where believers are experiencing unprecedented revival, in every case, I find a people who make prayer a top priority. A few years ago, I was ministering in Manaus, Brazil, where 10,000 new believers had been baptized in one day just a few months before I arrived. The Church in Manaus was experiencing revival of this magnitude as a result of passionate prayer.

I have been privileged to minister to some of the most influential leaders of the underground Church in China. I noticed that leaders of these underground congregations came one-half hour early to each meeting to pray. No one asked them to come. They just came and stood and prayed fervently for at least 30 minutes before our meetings began. It should be no surprise that more than 25,000 are coming to faith in Christ every day in the nation of China! The Christians there have learned to pray.

A few years ago, I was in South Africa, near Johannesburg, where people were giving their lives to Christ every week at every service. The pastor invited me to join him so I could experience the secret of the revival. An hour before the service, the pastor walked around the auditorium as hundreds followed him, crying out to the Lord in prayer.

Everywhere I see God moving in a sovereign way, I also see a common thread: prayer! Prior to these revivals and sovereign moves of God, God's people have learned to pray. And yet, Christians often struggle with their prayer lives more than any other area.

The Model Prayer

One day, after returning from Uzbekistan, I was reading the Scriptures and received a revelation from the book of Luke that changed my life. I noticed that Jesus' disciples seemed to have the same problem that many of us have of not knowing how to pray properly. In Luke 11:1, one of His disciples came to Jesus with a request: "Lord, teach us to pray." This is the only thing that Jesus' disciples ever asked Him to teach them. They knew that Jesus' prayer life was pivotal to everything else He did.

Jesus carried the presence of His heavenly Father with Him because of His intimate prayer life. He could perform miracles and heal the sick and cast out demons because He knew how to pray. Because He was totally committed to doing only that which He saw His heavenly Father doing, it had been essential that He learn to hear His Father's voice through prayer.

The disciples really wanted to know how to pray, just like their Master. They witnessed Jesus praying often and consistently:

> Before daybreak the next morning, Jesus got up and went out to an isolated place to pray (Mark 1:35).

> One day soon afterward Jesus went up on a mountain to pray, and he prayed to God all night (Luke 6:12).

> But Jesus often withdrew to the wilderness for prayer (Luke 5:16).

The disciples also saw the results of Jesus' devotion to spending time each morning with His heavenly Father; they had no doubt that His fervent prayer life was the reason Jesus could speak with such authority and wisdom, as the miracles literally flowed from His life.

What did Jesus say to the disciple's question? His immediate response was, "This is how you should pray." And then He prayed the Lord's Prayer as a model for praying (see Luke 11:2-4). Obviously, Jesus did not intend for His disciples (or us) to repeat this prayer by rote. This prayer is not about rules or how to be spiritually correct. It is about a relationship with the Lord and how to connect with Him. Then it dawned on me that the petitions we find in this prayer are there to serve as a model—a template, if you will. And this template is designed to express the *manner* in which we are to pray to our heavenly Father.

I remembered another Scripture, Isaiah 56:7, which says, "I will . . . give them joy in my house of prayer . . . for my house will be called a house of prayer for all nations" (*NIV*). Since I am the temple of the Holy Spirit (see 1 Cor. 3:16), I realized that I am the house of God. My body is God's house. Christ lives in me. The Lord then began to show me that He has called me to become a personal house of prayer—and He gave me a visual picture of a house. Not just any house, but a house with a courtyard in the center and twelve rooms all around it.

In Psalm 100:4 we read, "Enter his gates with thanksgiving; go into his courts with praise. Give thanks to him and praise his name." To extend the metaphor a little further, I find it profoundly helpful, as I come to a time of prayer, to actually see myself entering a building—a house—with thanksgiving. I actually envision rooms in this house.

The understanding the Lord gave to me about the Lord's Prayer is that it has twelve key parts, and I picture twelve rooms in that house, each one corresponding to a part of the prayer. In my mind, I enter this courtyard, which gives me access to twelve rooms—twelve different ways to pray—based on the model of the Lord Jesus.

What are the twelve rooms of prayer? In an abbreviated fashion, they are as follows:

1. The Family Room—Our Father in heaven,
2. The Adoration Room—hallowed be Your name.
3. The Declaration Room—Your Kingdom come.
4. The Surrender Room—Your will be done, on Earth as it is in heaven.
5. The Provision Room—Give us today our daily bread.
6. The Forgiveness Room—Forgive us our debts,

7. The Freedom Room—as we also have forgiven our debtors.
8. The Protection Room—And lead us not into temptation,
9. The Warfare Room—but deliver us from the evil one.
10. The Kingdom Room—For Yours is the Kingdom
11. The Power Room—and the power
12. The Exaltation Room—and the glory forever. Amen.[1]

Let's be clear, this is not about a form or a method. It is about receiving a revelation from God to become a personal house of prayer. It is about a relationship with a loving heavenly Father who desires to spend personal time with us each day. It is about spending time with Him in various rooms of prayer as you are led by the Holy Spirit each day.

My guess is that if you are not spending enough quality time with God each day the reason is not that you do not want to; you simply have not known how to. I have wonderful news for you: You can enter into a whole new world in prayer, and it will bring great joy to your life! I have found that Jesus gave us the Lord's Prayer as a model for prayer because He wants our very lives to become "houses of prayer." The Lord's Prayer teaches us how to become a personal house of prayer. It is our manual to learn how to pray according to the example of Jesus.

I have learned that believers all over the world and many of the Church fathers down through history have used the Lord's Prayer as a guide to teach them to pray. In the very earliest Christian documents, we find the praying of the Lord's Prayer taught and encouraged. In the writings of the Church fathers, we find its meaning drawn out and taught over and over again. Throughout the ages, the Church has known that disciples need to be taught to pray according to the pattern and model given by Jesus and passed on by the apostles.

The first-century rabbis usually instructed their students by giving them an outline of certain topics of truth. Then the rabbis taught from each point on this outline. In His model prayer, Jesus gives an outline of various topics and instructs His disciples: "This, then, is how you should pray . . ." (Matt. 6:9, *NIV*).

Our God is a God of patterns and plans. He gave Moses plans to build the tabernacle, and later He gave Solomon plans to build the temple. Generations later still, He gave us the plan for salvation through His Son, Jesus Christ. In the Lord's Prayer, He has given to us a plan that focuses on twelve different aspects of prayer to help us as we spend time with Him. Perhaps your personal intimate daily time of prayer with your heavenly Father is fulfilling just the way it is. If that is the case, then this approach may not be for you. But it is an option for those who feel they need help in their times of daily prayer.

Prayer is a relationship with a holy God who loves us, not a form to follow. However, relationship does not preclude planning. I have a healthy, growing love relationship with my wife, LaVerne, after 39 years of marriage, in part because there are certain plans and patterns God has helped me institute in our marriage over the years that have kept our relationship fresh and exciting. I plan date nights and times away with LaVerne on a regular basis because I love her; I don't do it out of legalism or obligation. This enhances our relationship. Our Master, Jesus, has given us, in the Lord's Prayer, a plan and a pattern to enhance our relationship with our heavenly Father. Putting that plan into practice will bring great joy in our times alone with Him.

Again I must emphasize that praying through the Lord's Prayer cannot become a legalistic approach to prayer. It is simply a template that can help you. It has helped me, and I am able to say that God has brought me to a place where I go to bed at night and can't wait to get up in the morning so I can spend time with Jesus. Praying and seeking the face of Jesus has become a joy, as it should be, as I meet with my best friend each day.

This revelation has revolutionized my prayer life. For more about how you can use the outline of the Lord's Prayer to take you into God's presence and satisfy your hunger to know Him and be in relationship with Him, I invite you to read my book, *Building Your Personal House of Prayer.*[2]

Devotional Discipleship

If you are reading this book, obviously God has stirred your heart to want more of Him. The great thing about God is that His arms are open wide to bring us into that place of intimate devotion that leads to daily abiding with Him. As a young believer, my (Jimmy's) greatest frustration was people telling me that I should pray or spend time with Jesus but not telling me how to do it.

So, how do we really disciple people to connect with God? I call it "life-on-life." Basically, I model connecting with God with the other person so he or she can see how it is done, learn it, and then pass it on to another person. When we spend time helping people learn how to engage God, we find not only that they can do it but that they are made for it.

Several years ago, I began a process I continue today of spending time with Jesus along with the people I am investing in. I use a basic structure of worship, Word and prayer. I start by worshiping the Lord by singing a song or quoting Scripture. The goal is to focus my heart on Jesus and rejoice in God's goodness and His faithfulness to fulfill His promises. I meditate on the Father, Son and Holy Spirit. In doing this, I have found a few Scriptures, such as Psalm 139:13-17, Hebrews 1:1-3, and John 16:7-16 to be helpful with this. Then I pray for the following:

- Intimacy with Christ: power to walk with God
- Family: parents, children, spouse, siblings
- Those in authority over me: small-group leaders, church leaders, government leaders
- Peers: people in my group, friends, roommates, classmates, co-workers
- Unreached people: the unreached nations of the world and those I know who don't know Jesus personally— I pray that the veil of unbelief would be lifted from their eyes, taking away any strongholds that would keep them from knowing Christ.

To follow this model, begin by spending some time learning to listen to the Lord. Ask God if there is anyone you need to encourage or if there is any area of your life that isn't totally submitted to Him. Keep a journal noting what God is saying to you. Next, read and memorize His Word. Start by reading one chapter in the Old Testament and one in the New Testament. Pick a Scripture verse or passage to memorize each week and recite it daily. Always end your time praising God and thanking Him for His goodness.

A few years ago James Mark and Noel, two members of my church, came to me and said that they were frustrated with the lack of consistency in their devotional lives and needed help. So I said, "Meet me at my office at 5:30 A.M. and be willing to spend an hour with me learning how to spend time with Jesus.

We will meet every day for five days, and then I think you'll have what you need to go forward."

So on Day 1, I had my time with Jesus with them. I recited Scriptures about who the Father is, who Jesus is and who the Holy Spirit is. I shared my meditative thoughts. We worshiped together, and then we sat down together and read a portion of the Bible. I prayed through my prayer list, and they heard me sharing Scriptures for each person.

We continued meeting together each day. At the end of our time each morning, we prayed over our days, in specifics, waited on God by journaling together and then they would leave. Each day I would have them do one part a little bit more on their own. By the fifth day, we were all in our separate rooms, spending time with Jesus. They were now able to bring clarity to the things that were in their hearts. To this day, they consider this experience to be a life-changing experience, because they not only heard about it from others but also experienced it for themselves.

Throughout our movement around the world, people use this as a discipleship model to help people engage God and build a lifestyle of intimate fellowship with Him. There are thousands of people who can have an effective time with Jesus, not just because someone told them to but also because they modeled it for them in life-on-life relationship.

This works at every age level. Because of our passion for people to meet with Jesus to get their needs met in God alone, we train children, youth, college students and adults at every age level. We not only believe you can do it, but we also believe it is essential for your life.

In our own family, Laura and I have modeled this for our children at every stage of their development. When they were little and could not read, we read the Bible to them. We prayed for them, and as soon as they could form words we taught them Scriptures and had them pray as well. We introduced Bible stories through videos, which we called "quiet time videos." While we spent our own time with Jesus, our children would watch these 20- to 30-minute presentations about the life of Jesus. Afterwards, we talked about the stories they had just heard, and we prayed together. As soon as they could read their first words, our kids began to spend time alone with Jesus. We taught them how to read the Bible, how to worship, and how to pray—often sitting by their sides and helping them through that process.

Today, as I write this, my children are 20, 17, 15 and 11 years old. Every day, they spend time in the Word, worship and prayer—not out of duty, not because they have to, but out of a delight and a desire to meet with God. Laura and I have not only modeled this, but our family has lived it out together, whether we are on vacation, at retreats or on weekend getaways—wherever we are, we all spend time with Jesus to start our days, because apart from Him, we can do nothing, and apart from Him, we don't want to do anything.

To love Jesus is to long to be with Him, but that longing is not enough. There is a need to structure our lives around spending time with Him. Another way that you could say it is "desire ➤ discipline ➤ delight," because that progression captures the essence of what it takes to develop a consistent devotional life. You can be motivated with great desire, but without discipline you will never get there. Discipline positions us to receive grace. Discipline is not the grace; it is the submission of our heart to encounter the grace of God. It is not about whether God loves us—His love is sure whether we are disciplined or not—but it is our wholehearted response to Him that allows us to find Him.

"For I know the plans that I have for you," declares the Lord, "plans for welfare and not for calamity to give you a future and a hope. Then you will call upon Me and come and pray to Me, and I will listen to you. You will seek Me and find Me when you search for Me with all your heart. I will be found by you," declares the Lord (Jer. 29:11-14, *NASB*).

Jesus wants us to find Him. He wants to reveal Himself to us, but there has to be submission of our lives in order to get to that place of delight and experiencing the fullness of all that He has for us.

Several years ago, our church did a survey and discovered there were three things that kept people from spending an hour alone with Jesus each morning: "I am too sleepy," "I am too tired," and "I don't see the benefit." As I worked to unpack this survey, I began to think through how to help people with those challenges.

For instance, if you are too sleepy to spend time with the Lord in the morning, my first recommendation is to go to bed earlier. Probably the news and David Letterman are not what your soul needs to feel refreshed and renewed in God. If you are "too sleepy" for a morning devotion, I encourage you to order your time in a way that will allow you to go to bed early enough that you can start your day with the Lord.

If you need help getting up early, have an accountability partner who knows you well enough to not let you pull any tricks. For years I had a friend who called me at 5:00 every morning to wake me up. I had chosen that time to start my time with God each morning, but when my friend called I would answer and then hang up and go back to sleep. So I told him to ask me if I was actually out of the bed. Then, when I began falling asleep in my chair, I had him ask if I was sitting in the white chair. Eventually, I had to get up and immediately go for a walk out-side—all while still on the phone. Once I started walking and praying outside, I had high motivation to not fall asleep onto the cement! I told my friend all of my tricks in order to disci-pline my life. These little things began to keep me awake enough to begin to pray and to experience God. Walking was my first step in waking up to a life of prayer and intercession.

After walking and praying, I was awake enough when I re-turned to read the Word and allow it to become life to me. I had a disciplined process of reading a psalm, a proverb, and then two or three chapters from the Bible. This daily reading allowed God to speak to me consistently, not just on one issue but on the multiple issues of life.

God is inviting you to experience the adventure of a life-time by living in His presence. But you must do whatever it takes to enter into that adventure. Don't kid yourself that sim-ply setting your alarm and having a desire will end up giving you that time that is so needful for your life to be renewed and refreshed and for God to do all that He wants to do in your life. May you seek Him not just with *desire* but also with a *discipline* that will allow you to live a life of absolute *delight*.

Notes

1. See Appendix A for a diagram of the 12 rooms and more about entering each room to commune with Jesus.

2. Larry Kreider, *Building Your Personal House of Prayer* (Shippensburg, PA: Destiny Im-age Publications, 2008).

LOVING HIS
PEOPLE

5

Loving God's People

Why we are so passionate about loving people, pouring our lives into them, and fulfilling our call to become spiritual fathers and mothers

Starting in the early 1970s, I (Larry) got my first real introduction to loving people and very much wanting to see them succeed in their Christian lives. As I previously mentioned, I helped to start a youth ministry with a small band of young adults who began to reach out to the youth of our community. The friendship evangelism produced results, and during the next few years, dozens of young people came to faith in Christ.

Every Sunday, we took vanloads of these new believers to visit various churches in our community, because we wanted to help them find their place in a local church. After the church services, the entire group usually returned to our home for a time of praise, prayer, spiritual counseling and just plain fun. Before long, some of the other leaders asked me to begin a weekly Bible study to nurture these new believers. Our desire was to teach them from the Scriptures what practical Christian living was really all about and to assist them in being planted in a local church so they could grow and flourish in their Christian lives.

We soon discovered that these kids offered a challenge for the local churches, and vice versa. Although the believers in the local churches were friendly and helpful, something wasn't clicking. These young believers simply were not being incorporated into the life of the established churches in our communities. Some of the young believers were getting married and starting families of their own, but they were unable to feel at home within the existing church structures. Our goal of trying to assimilate the kids into the Body of Christ in our community was failing.

To remedy this problem, my wife, LaVerne, and I began to develop what we called Paul-Timothy discipling relationships with the new Christians. I met with a few young men each week for Bible study and prayer, and LaVerne did the same with young women. Early on, we realized these relationships were going to be a work in progress, and it might be a long time before we saw spectacular results. Many of the kids came from one particular neighborhood where motorcycle gangs and drugs were commonplace. Since most of the kids were first-generation believers, they received little support from friends and family.

We were young ourselves, didn't know much, and made mistakes, but we loved Jesus with all our hearts and believed we needed to give our lives sacrificially for these kids. We knew that in order for these young believers to grow spiritually and not fall away, we would have to do more than spend time in a discipleship-type Bible study with them. They needed to see Christianity practically modeled and working, or none of it would make any sense to them. We didn't call it mentoring or spiritual parenting at the time, but we were doing it just the same. It was more than a duty or event for us; it was a lifestyle of being connected in relationship with younger Christians who desperately needed supportive, nurturing commitment from older Christians.

We opened our hearts and home to these kids and loved them unconditionally. Deep down we realized that if we coached them to grow up spiritually, they could someday help others, and it would all be worth it (although in all honesty we didn't consciously see that far ahead at the time). So we welcomed these teenagers into our daily lives. They spent a lot of time hanging out at our house, creating permanent red Kool-Aid stains on the carpet, and occasionally punching holes in the wall during wrestling matches.

Most of the training took place as they observed us lovingly disciplining our children or fixing that persistent roof leak. We were learning step by step how to be effective spiritual parents, and they were learning how to bear fruit as Christians.

The Lord was faithful. Out of these inauspicious beginnings, a church was birthed with some of these young believers who were being trained to take on the next batch of spiritual children. It was during this time that God spoke to me and asked if I was willing to be involved in an "underground church." Although baffled at first, I began to understand that an underground church would consist of small groups of believers meeting in homes to pray, evangelize and build relationships with one another. As water and nutrients feed the tree by climbing up through the root system, so the Church is nourished and strengthened by what happens in the underground, or less-seen realm of church life—believers involved in relationships in small groups. I realized that most of the work of ministry—prayer, study, relationship building and outreach—would take place in the context of these home meetings. Because of the size of these home groups, every member of the church is empowered to embrace the vital role they are to play as a member of the greater church body. Being well nourished and active in the ministry, each member serves as a powerful building block of the church. Small groups remind us of our calling to do ministry, and they also provide opportunities for that ministry.

In 1980, a group of approximately 25 believers met for the first time for a Sunday morning celebration in a living room. During the next 10 years, DOVE Christian Fellowship grew to include well over 2,000 believers scattered throughout communities in a seven-county area of Pennsylvania. We met in more than 100 small groups during the week, and on Sunday mornings we came together in larger congregations in five different locations.

We realized that as people are trained, they should be released (or given away) to start new churches. Equipping people and allowing them to move out on their own affords limitless potential. It became clear to us that in order for DOVE Christian Fellowship to accomplish what God had called us to do, we needed to adjust our church government and be willing to give the church away.

So we did just that. We turned over the leadership and ministry of the church to 8 pastors, 21 elders, and a whole host of small-group leaders. In 1996, the church decentralized and became eight cell-based churches, and I was asked to serve as its international director. There were three other churches—congregations we had helped to start in Kenya, Uganda and New Zealand—who joined our new family of churches. Today, the DOVE family includes many thousands of believers serving with more than 150 churches in the nations of Barbados, Brazil, Bulgaria, Canada, Guatemala, Haiti, India, Kenya, the

Netherlands, New Zealand, Peru, Rwanda, Scotland, South Africa, Uganda and the United States.

This means we have had the privilege, at DOVE Christian Fellowship International (DCFI), of watching many of our spiritual children, grandchildren, and great-grandchildren reproduce spiritual sons and daughters as new small groups and new churches are planted throughout the world.[1]

There was nothing special about us, and there still isn't! We were ordinary young people, made lots of mistakes, and have many stories to tell that are not success stories, but we had the hearts of parents to teach their children. We loved Jesus, we really loved those kids, and as any parent would, we expected them to grow! Spiritual parenting was a key in helping that to happen. Our God is a God of family—a God of relationship—and He is our Father. He has called us to imitate Him by becoming spiritual fathers and mothers ourselves and by loving His people, just as He does.

Here's one spiritual parenting story that is typical of what happens when someone takes the time to mentor another person in his or her walk with God. Betty and Holly, from a DOVE church in Pennsylvania, began their spiritual mother-daughter relationship over coffee, eggs and toast. This relationship came at a time of deep need in Holly's life. She recalls, "The Lord chose Betty to stand in the gap to help meet the needs of a hurting child crying out in a woman's body. Betty is a Proverbs 31 woman. She is not a woman who takes any glory; it all goes to the Lord. She practices what she preaches. She never betrays my trust or gossips. If she makes a mistake, she humbles herself and admits it. I have a lot of love and respect for her obedience to God."

During their mentoring relationship, Betty visited Holly once a week and called her a few times a week. And Holly called

Betty. During the first few months of mentoring, Betty worked with Holly on being consistent in her walk with the Lord and encouraged her to read a book called *The Normal Christian Life*. Says Holly:

> I have always had a problem reading, and it was difficult to understand. So one day I thought I could outsmart her. I was in the hospital for minor surgery and purposely left the book at the hospital (to benefit another person's soul!). Well, the next time Betty came to my house, she had two copies of the book. She was definitely on to me! So we sat down and finished the book together. Sometimes I had tears of frustration in my eyes because this book was so difficult for me, but Betty believed in me and didn't allow me to give up on myself.
>
> She often spoke the truth in love to me. Sometimes I would ask her if she was mad at me. She would say, "No, Holly, I'm just being salty." She was very careful throughout our friendship not to have me become dependent on her. She knew my dependence had to be on the Lord Jesus Christ. The relationship became closer because I could trust her. Early on in our talks, she said I could use her as a "human garbage disposal." I've shared with her my deepest, most intimate secrets. I believe spiritual parenting is so important in churches today. There are too many broken homes. Men and women are growing up without proper spiritual training or godly love and nurturing. For example, I am 27 years old and never learned how to cook before. Betty has shown me how to cook meals on many occasions. Afterwards, we would sit down and read Scriptures or have

prayer together. She integrated two parts of being a spiritual parent—one part being an earthly parent with the cooking and the other with reading the Word of God.

Betty and I come from two different families, different circumstances, different looks, and believe me, we do not always agree on the same things. Isn't that the way mother and daughter relationships are? My point is that it is not wrong to be different. It is the love of Jesus that brings us together because we come from the same God who created us all. Betty does not judge me because of my past and always encourages me to go forward toward the prize for the better things God has for me.

Pour Your Life into Others

We are both totally convinced that there is a desperate need in today's Church for spiritually mature men and women to mentor younger believers to be fully equipped and faithful servants of Christ. That's why I (Larry) wrote a book on returning to the biblical truth of spiritual parenting titled *Authentic Spiritual Mentoring*.[2] I believe that mentoring is an important part of the discipleship formation strategy of Jesus and that investment in others will pay great dividends in the form of a multiplied spiritual legacy. As a disciple-maker, you can influence countless others and impact the world as you make an investment that keeps on growing. If you mentor one person who disciples another, and that one person disciples yet another, and those persons each mentor one person, the multiplication effects are astounding!

No matter what you do vocationally—whether you are a housewife, a student, a worker in a factory, a pastor of a church, a missionary, or the head of a large corporation—you have the divine responsibility to birth spiritual children, grandchildren and great-grandchildren. Your legacy will be all the spiritual children that you can someday present to Jesus Christ.

Several years ago, I was in Barbados training church leaders and believers on the subject of spiritual parenting. The day I was to come back to the United States, Bill Landis, a missionary who leads Youth With A Mission's Caribbean ministry, invited me to come to his home before going to the airport. Bill and his family, along with a team of leaders, were in the process of equipping Bajan Christians to become spiritual leaders. On this visit to his house, Bill told me some interesting history about this tiny island nation. He explained that, years ago, many people were brought as slaves to Barbados from various places in West Africa, including the nation of Gambia. Now, Bill and his team are training Bajan Christians as missionaries so that they can return to their ancestral country of Gambia and lead Muslim Gambians to Christ. With a common heritage, it is the ideal match.

Then Bill said something that moved me deeply: "Larry, do you realize the people being reached in Gambia are a part of your spiritual heritage? You were one of my spiritual fathers, so you have a part in the ongoing legacy."

As I sat on the plane returning to the United States, I was overwhelmed at the significance of Bill's words. Years ago, long before I was a pastor or an author or a church leader, I was a young man on a chicken farm who led a Bible study of young people. During that time, I was a spiritual father to Bill. Bill was a spiritual father to those he had discipled in Barbados.

The Bajan Christians who were now going to Africa to lead Gambians to Christ were like my spiritual grandchildren, and the spiritual children they birthed and nurtured in Gambia would be my great-grandchildren. Generations to come would receive God's promises because a chicken farmer had been obedient to God's call to disciple a bunch of rambunctious teenagers more than 30 years ago. Yes, this was part of my spiritual legacy. As I pondered this reality, I was deeply moved. I was privileged to share a large inheritance that had multiplied beyond my wildest dreams!

I was reminded in that moment that God takes ordinary people who love Jesus and transforms them by His presence. God can use us to mentor others at any point in our Christian walks if we allow Him free rein in our lives.

It's an Investment

As a young college student, I (Jimmy) spent time with Bob Stuplich at Mountain Ministries in Colorado. Bob took me to a meeting where his pastor was sharing about the power and influence of men in our lives. He went around the room and asked us to name an influential man in our lives. As they got closer to me, I didn't know what I was going to say. I was trying to think of a man who had influenced me significantly outside of my own family, but I couldn't come up with anybody. Before they landed on me, I decided to name Bob because my few days with him had made a great impact on me. However, the group ran out of time before I had to share.

Even though I didn't have to answer the question at the meeting, my inability to come up with one man who had invested in my life really troubled me. I told Bob what was bothering me. His answer was, "I think it is an indictment of my generation because we didn't value investing in those coming up behind us. We climbed the ladder of success but never took the time or made it a priority to invest in younger men's lives. Why don't you pray and ask God to bring men into your life? I think He will do that."

I prayed that prayer in the spring of 1985. Since that time, God has provided many fathers and mothers in the Lord who have profoundly affected who I am and how I live my life. Fred Piepman, a missionary I worked with in New Guinea, was among the first answers to that prayer. Fred was a true father in the faith. He taught me how to hear from God, to believe in the supernatural, to learn by doing, to trust God completely with my finances, and to be a godly man who loves his wife and family and not just the work of the ministry.

I came out of my time in New Guinea with an even firmer conviction of life-on-life ministry. To me, that means that discipleship is the way Jesus raised up His leaders and the way they raised up their leaders. Paul said to Timothy, "The things which you have heard from me in the presence of many witnesses, entrust these to faithful men who will be able to teach others also" (2 Tim. 2:2, *NASB*). This is the way that lives are changed.

Build from the Bottom Up

Soon after my time in New Guinea as a college student, God spoke to me, maybe more clearly than I've ever heard. He said, "I want you to stay and watch Me build My Church from the bottom up." I really had no idea what that meant, nor did I have any way to do that from my perspective, but I knew that God had spoken. His words to me were especially significant because they confirmed something He had planted in my heart through another spiritual father He had provided for me—Robert Ewing. Robert and his family had been a part of the spiritual awakening in Waco in the late 1940s, and Robert had developed a deep love for the Church. He later became the leader of a ministry team charged with overseeing 80 churches around the world.

Robert opened his life to me, teaching and mentoring me in the faith. I loved going to his house for lunch and hearing his stories about dramatic healings, miracles and smuggling Bibles into closed countries. His work inspired me to believe God for the impossible. Robert would talk for hours about the Church. He was convinced that it was God's instrument to change the world. As he talked about the different Scripture passages that speak about God's design and desire to see the Church be all that it is called to be, my heart was set afire. This was the dream that I was willing to live and die for: that God would be glorified in the earth through His Church. If we could learn to be the Church and reproduce the Church around the world, then the glory of God would be seen in every tribe, tongue, people and nation. The days I spent learning from Robert deeply shaped who I am today and my love for the Church.

In the late 1980s, Mark, the college pastor of our church at the time, went to the elders and gave them a proposal: What if the local church created a process of evangelism, discipleship and reproducing our lives that eventually would affect our city, our nation and the nations of the world? The elders accepted the proposal with joy and sent us on our journey. Just as others had invested in us, Laura and I began to invest in men and women. At one time, I had up to 16 one-hour appointments each week, investing in people's lives so they could go and do the same. Little by little, we saw the process begin to work.

After three years of investing in lives and creating mission opportunities, I eventually became the college pastor. We gathered the people we had been discipling and said, "Why don't you join together with us, and let's learn how to do discipleship in a much larger way. Our basic model is this: Everything that has life reproduces itself. If I meet with Jesus and He changes my life, then I invest in others and Jesus changes their lives, and they are able to see Jesus change others' lives. That group becomes more small groups, which eventually become a church, and then that church eventually becomes many churches, which can affect the whole world." Life-on-life discipleship through small-group community became the core of everything we do in order to reach the nations.

One of the first people I discipled, a young man named Kurt, came to me as a graduate student, confessing his sins and unburdening the weight of darkness in his life. As he did this, he experienced an incredible, fresh relationship with God that he couldn't help but share with others. He began sharing the gospel and intentionally investing in others, just as I was investing in him. He and his future wife, Karen, became a part of our original core team. They began to pray and seek God on a weekly basis, asking, "How do we do this not just on an individual level but as Acts 2 communities?"

Kurt began to invest in people and see their lives transformed as they were set free of besetting sins. Not only did he and Karen have a heart for nations, but they also invested in others who had the same heart for the nations. Years later, we looked back and realized that Kurt had discipled our team leader in Uzbekistan, who later became our team leader in Tunisia. Kurt also invested in our team leader in Afghanistan and a man named Neil who is planting one of our granddaughter churches in the Boston area. Between them, he and his wife have affected hundreds, if not thousands, of people through their intentional investment of love and life. Not only did they live out the values themselves, but they also invested in others—not just individually but as reproducing small groups for the kingdom of God.

We began focusing small groups specifically on discipling young men and women. Out of this commitment to teaching discipleship, as well as modeling it, we saw a whole new wave of leaders emerge, many of whom are planting churches and leading our local ministries today. These young leaders, along with so many others, partnered with us during those days to lead, disciple, and reproduce their lives. I could spend days listing names of people all around the world whose lives have been influenced as a direct result of this season of discipleship.

Through our church in Waco, Texas, and our church plants in the United States and overseas, we have seen thousands of people reproduce small groups all over the world through the discipleship process. As we recently sought God on His direction for the next 20 years, we asked the question, "What is the one factor that will allow us to continue to grow and be effective in the world?" That one thing is discipleship. If discipleship happens, then everything else happens. If discipleship doesn't happen, all will eventually unravel. It is that life-on-life investment that changes the world. We have people from the ages of 7 to 70 investing in others—sharing their lives and their love of Jesus. Businessmen disciple other businessmen over lunch, ladies meet for morning coffee to share their hearts, children share their love of Jesus on the playground, and the list goes on. It was the plan of Jesus, and it should be our plan as well.

Our School of Tyrannus

During the mid 1990s, DOVE went through a season of introspection as a church. We felt we had made many mistakes.

Although thousands of lives had been changed by Jesus, we longed for more. Jim and Judy Orred, from Youth With A Mission in the Balkans, and their family took a sabbatical and came to live for five months in Lancaster County, Pennsylvania, where they connected with our church. They were so encouraging and insightful. One day Jim asked me, "Larry, why don't you have a leadership training school?"

I replied quickly, "Because we have made too many mistakes."

He simply replied, "That's why you need a school—so others you are discipling and training do not make the same mistakes you have made." He was right! We needed to continue to train the next generation of leaders one on one in discipleship relationships as we had been doing, but we also needed a training school to prepare a whole new crop of church planters and missionaries for the nations.

We saw in Acts 19:9 that Paul took the disciples with him and had discussions daily in the School of Tyrannus. We felt like we needed our own "School of Tyrannus." So the DOVE Church Planting and Leadership School was born.

Today, after more than 15 years, this school has been used in many places throughout the world to train hundreds of leaders in our family of churches and in the larger Body of Christ. We have physical campuses in various locations and a video training program used around the world. This school was recently renamed the DOVE Leadership Training School, but it still has a strong emphasis on planting new churches in our nation and in the nations.

Chad's story is one of many examples of someone who has been discipled and then trained in our school. Chad and Chris are a young couple who grew up in our church. They were small-group leaders who fell in love, got married, and went on a short-term mission trip to northeast Brazil. After they returned home, they felt called by God to return to northeast Brazil to learn to speak Portuguese and then to reach kids on the streets with the love of Jesus, disciple them, and start a new church. Chad and Chris sold their home, took the DOVE Leadership Training School course for practical training in church planting, and continued to grow in the Lord's passion to reach the lost and make disciples. They followed His call to minister in northeastern Brazil, where they would learn a new language, live within a new and unfamiliar culture, make new friends, and most of all take the gospel of Jesus Christ to a needy nation.

Leaving a growing and thriving family business, an effective youth ministry at their church, lots of friends, and all the comforts of home, Chad and Chris were obedient to follow God into a city of four million people, Fortaleza, and start building a life and ministry there. They quickly learned that church planting must be birthed in prayer for it to be fruitful. They had a strategy for reaching young people and rapidly developed rapport with them. God tremendously blessed them, and many youth found new life in Christ. Their daily discipleship and weekly meetings in their home drew in parents and other adults seeking God. They soon started a thriving church called Comunidade Cristã DOVE, in Forteleza, Brazil. They also had a vision to open a youth center as well as establish a business venture that would enable them to provide much-needed income for many poor families with whom they connected.

At one point in their church-planting adventure, members of Comunidade Cristã DOVE joined with a local restaurant owner to set up a soup kitchen for the needy. On the first day of the soup kitchen, the restaurant owner, with a very worried look on her face, said to Chad, "I made soup for 50, but there are at least 120 people here! Should we just fill up half of the cups?"

Chad felt the Lord say that there would be enough for everyone. Everyone got in line, and the servers started filling cups. As the end of the line neared, they noticed that they still didn't hear the ladle scraping the bottom of the pan. After everyone had a cup full of soup, Chad asked if there was any soup left. One of the servers smiled and said, "I'm not sure what is happening here, but this pan is still half-filled with soup!" Chad called everyone to get in line again and get another cup of soup. After that, the ladle still wasn't scraping the bottom.

So Chad called for whoever was still hungry to get in line one more time, and those 15-year-old boys (who seemed to have bottomless pits in their stomachs) got in line again. Only after everyone was so full that they just couldn't eat any more did that ladle start scraping the bottom. They had experienced a miracle of Jesus multiplying the soup!

After the meal, a teenager who was a new Christian gave his testimony, along with an invitation to anyone who wanted to receive Christ. Six women came forward in tears, eager to give their lives to the Lord.

Miracles and salvation experiences were commonplace as the Spirit of God moved to free many in the community from the bondage of the enemy. After eight years, Chad and Chris Miller turned the church over to national leaders and returned to the United States. Today, Chad and Chris serve as spiritual parents to the leadership of this healthy Brazilian church and continue to mentor them weekly via Skype and by taking trips on a regular basis to Fortaleza. And they often take with them teams of youth and young adults who also receive a vision from God to plant churches in the nations. The vision continues.

Chad currently serves as the youth director for DOVE USA churches, training youth leaders throughout America.

Fruitful but Fragile

A couple of times a year, our (Antioch's) church leadership gathers to pray through vision and direction for the upcoming year. We spend time seeking God together and talking through implementation.

In 2004, as I (Jimmy) was asking God about this upcoming time together, He spoke to me this simple phrase: *We are fruitful, but fragile.* I realized that in seeing God work in incredible ways over the years, we had become part of a movement. We were no longer just a church that plants churches, but a movement of people with like hearts and minds, and with similar values that were touching people all around the world. God was blessing us with much fruit. But, though we were fruitful, we were also fragile.

We are fragile on two levels. First, we are fragile in the sense that we have focused our lives and ministries around our intimate day-to-day walks with Jesus. If at any time we lose that sensitivity, that daily personal devotion, that worship and honor of Him in every aspect of our lives, we could quickly fall apart. If there is anything that has kept us on track, it is seeking Him daily, listening to Him, and responding to Him in every way.

The second thing that makes us fragile is that we have committed ourselves to relationships. We have built a worldwide relational network that is both wonderful and difficult. As we invest wholeheartedly in our people's lives, we are constantly sending them off to serve around the world and then welcoming new people in. It is hard at times to keep up with everything and everybody. God admonishes us over and over again to love one another, forgive one another, restore one another, and speak truth to one another. All the "one another" commands of Scripture need to be in operation in our midst.

When we commit ourselves to relational ministry, there are always conflicts to resolve, people to help, misunderstandings to clarify, and teams to develop. Sometimes it seems like it would be easier to set up a structure of hiring and firing people, but God hasn't called us to that kind of life. He has called us to a type of organic life that will cost us everything, while causing us to continue to grow in love and be changed by the grace of God. This life-on-life discipleship and small-group ministry has made us very fruitful, but also very fragile.

In a statement: We are in it for Him, and we are in it for them.

We want to love, honor and glorify Jesus, not just in the big things, but in every little thing, listening and responding to Him. When people come to us and celebrate what is happening around us, we can truly say that all glory goes to God because we have simply listened and responded to Him.

We are also in it for them. When the Bible says to love our neighbors as ourselves, we see that our calling is wrapped up in serving others. For us to get all of our inheritance in God, we have to be about other people getting their inheritance, too. There is no one person who can change the world, but a team of people who effectively seek the glory of God in their lives can. It truly is about Him and them. Whenever we lose sight of either, we miss out on what God has for us.

That's why we have home groups in our churches: to help fulfill this relational vision from our God to love His people. Or, to say it another way, our call from God could be stated simply like this: He has called us to build relationships with Jesus and with one another, and to reach the world from house to house, city to city, nation to nation. It is all about our relationship with Jesus and obeying His call to reach our world together with Him.

Notes
1. If you want to read more about our story at DOVE Christian Fellowship International, read the book I wrote about our church's adventure in small groups, entitled *House to House,* by Larry Kreider (Shippensburg, PA: Destiny Image Publishers, 2009).
2. Larry Kreider, *Authentic Spiritual Mentoring* (Ventura, CA: Regal Books, 2008).
3. If you want to read more about our story at Antioch Community Church, read the book I wrote, entitled *The Church Can Change the World,* by Jimmy Seibert (Charleston, SC: BookSurge Publishing, 2008).

6

Pouring Your Life into People

How to make loving God's people a priority and make disciples like Jesus, Paul and the New Testament believers did

Sara came to Baylor University and immediately got involved in a small group at nearby Antioch Community Church. She dove in with all her heart, living with people she met at church and eventually even leading her own group.

During her sophomore year, Sara's sister Shelly transferred to Baylor as well. Shelly had been making disastrous choices with partying, drugs and alcohol, but she hoped that moving to Waco would help her start a new life. However, shortly after transferring to Baylor, she found her life headed in the same old direction. Although she met many of Sara's small-group friends, this didn't keep her from a lifestyle that was leading her toward destruction.

Sara's heart broke for her sister, as did the hearts of many friends in her community. At one point, some of the small-group members felt like the Holy Spirit was impressing on them that Shelly was in a very dangerous place—that she was actually at the crossroads of making a decision between a journey that would lead her to death and the road that leads to life in Jesus. They decided to call a three-day fast on Shelly's behalf.

Things definitely did not look hopeful when Shelly showed up at the small-group leader's apartment and, in a very belligerent and scornful manner, said that she would never accept Jesus. In fact, Shelly even told Sara that she knew she was going to hell, and she was fine with that.

Although broken-hearted, Sara and the small-group community continued to believe for Shelly's life. Shelly seemed to take a turn for the worse when her boyfriend broke up with her. She threw herself fully into drugs, stopped eating, stopped sleeping, and was seemingly trying to destroy her life through partying.

It was during this time that Shelly, while on a drug high with another friend, mysteriously began talking about Jesus. Although it was very contradictory to the state she was in, she found herself talking about how Jesus was the only way to heaven. The more she talked, the more she became convinced. Finally she looked at her friend and said, "God is giving me another chance. I would be a fool not to accept His offer of a changed life."

Shelly left the apartment where she was doing drugs and went straight to her sister's place. Sara opened the door and was shocked to find Shelly broken, tender, and telling her that she wanted to give her life to the Lord. The small group celebrated that night as word got around that God had miraculously intervened at a time when things seemed the most hopeless.

The next week at our college service, the celebration was equal to a football team winning a national championship. People screamed and cheered. Shelly had invited many friends to come, because she wanted to share with them what God was doing in her life. She made sure, though, to distance herself from the ones who didn't want to change, so she wouldn't be influenced by them to get into more trouble.

Shelly's parents were so touched by her transformation that they began coming to Antioch even though they lived out of town. They had a heart to do mission work and decided that Antioch was the community that they wanted to be a part of. After going through the training school, they joined the staff and are now serving with Antioch as church planters in Japan. Sara also went through the training school. She served on our urban staff and is now a member of our team in India.

Today, Shelly is a vibrant part of our church plant in Seattle, Washington. A few years ago, she spent a summer in Peru, where she was able to lead many people to the Lord, boldly sharing her testimony of God's deliverance from drugs and a destructive lifestyle. Shelly and her whole family are being used powerfully by God to see lives transformed as they serve Him with all their hearts, reconciled to each other, and fully in love with Jesus.

People Investing in People

Ultimately, everything that has life reproduces itself. When an individual gets on fire for God, that person can't help but invest in other people. This produces a small group. When a small group grows together in the life of God, it can't help but bring more people in. Those small groups become churches. When those churches are obedient to the call Jesus gave His followers, they can't help but go to the nations with the gospel. Those churches reproduce and become more churches. When new churches catch the vision of their parent church, they too can't help but continue the work and plant even more churches. Church-plants reproduce even more churches and become movements.

Again, let us emphasize Paul's exhortation to Timothy: "The things which you have heard from me in the presence of many witnesses, entrust these to faithful men who will be able to teach others also" (2 Tim. 2:2, *NASB*). This is the way God's Kingdom has always worked: people investing in people, life on life, for the glory of God. Church must be a collection of strong discipleship relationships—not just one or two people, but hundreds who have invested in one another purposefully and intentionally. Over the years, this type of community creates a sense of family and maturity in the Body of Christ.

Early on, I (Jimmy) knew that it would take all the gifts Scripture speaks about if we were to become the people that God called us to be. But one thing we have taught our people is that no matter what your gift is, God has called us all to be abandoned to Him. Everybody should be earnestly seeking Jesus every day. No matter what our calling, all of us should be involved in discipleship. No matter how we serve, all of us should be involved in evangelism. All of us should be leading holy and sacrificial lives.

As we saw leaders emerge in our accounting department, administrative positions, pastoral roles, children's ministry, and worship ministry, we kept the same standards for everyone. All of us would live out the basic values of the Kingdom: loving God, discipleship, evangelism, being men and women of prayer, and living intentionally in the context of community. We wanted everyone in our community, from the secretaries to the musicians on stage, to be fully devoted followers of Christ. Keeping these standards has allowed us all to be of one heart and mind together. These commitments mark us and drive us, and it is through discipleship relationships that we will see them reproduced and lived out in generation after generation of new disciples.

As in all things that bear long-term fruit, there must be simple, biblically based, reproducible tools that help people pass on the words and teaching of Jesus, one to another. We've adapted seven basic discipleship lessons we call the "Foundations of Faith." Through life-on-life discipleship, you can impart these simple values of the Kingdom.

One man named Jason had grown up in poverty, abuse, gangs and drugs. He had been in jail, as had his sister, and his dad was currently in prison as well. Jason and his girlfriend, Monica, had a child and did drugs together until she left to raise their son on her own.

Jason continued to spiral downward, finally landing back in jail, where he became desperate and cried out to God. A new pastor in town started going to the jail in Lubbock and spent time with him. Upon Jason's release, this pastor encouraged him to visit Antioch. The first time Jason attended one of our services, Jim and Amy noticed he looked out of place and invited him to sit with them. They took him to lunch and invited him that night to Lifegroup. Soon after that, Jason and Monica started seeing each other again. Monica had had two other children while they were separated, and when they got back together, she became pregnant with twins.

Jim began meeting with Jason weekly, discipling him, while Amy met with Monica, gave her a baby shower, and found a rental house. Jason and Monica moved out of the projects with Amy's help and the grace of a man named Rick, who fixed up their house and bought them appliances. Rick showed amazing generosity and service to this needy family.

Jason always brought other broken people to the discipleship times, and eventually Jim and Amy began going through the "Foundations of Faith" with a group that met on Sunday nights in Jason and Monica's house. One couple, Rick and Donna, in their Sunday group came from Jason's work. Rick got saved the Sunday we showed a recording of Jason's story that we had made for the church service. He and Donna were baptized in the parking lot at our 20-year anniversary celebration. José, a childhood friend of Jason's, also got saved through this process and is also going through the lessons on Sunday nights.

This group now includes quite a few people, and they all sit together when they come to church. Amy said she and Jim love it—they have grandmas, singles, married couples, and ex-drug addicts growing in Jesus in their Lifegroup!

Discipleship Modeled

Jesus Himself modeled spiritual fathering and discipleship. Though He ministered to the multitudes, He spent most of His time on earth as a spiritual father to twelve men. He knew that Kingdom values were caught more than taught. He trained His disciples so they could grow up spiritually and be equipped to train others. He fished, prayed, wept and rejoiced with these disciples, and they went on to "father" many more people in the kingdom of God.

When Jesus trained His disciples, He didn't tell them how to be disciples by having them sit on a hill somewhere and lecturing them for three years. He taught them from real-life experiences as they traveled from place to place and actively learned, by Jesus' example and demonstration, about the kingdom of God. The disciples witnessed firsthand God's power and compassion when they came to Jesus for bread to feed a hungry multitude. They learned to discern the true from the false when Jesus exposed the scribes and Pharisees in their false piety and self-righteousness.

Jesus was totally accessible and approachable to His disciples for three years, and they grew spiritually mature under His tutelage. They were not perfect, but He believed in them enough to entrust the Church to them when He ascended into heaven.

As God's people, we all need help to grow up. It is very difficult to do it by ourselves, just as natural infants cannot thrive if left on their own. Just as babies need the care and nurture of parents, believers need practical input from more spiritually mature men and women who delight in their "children" reaching their full potential in Christ. They need spiritual parents to sow into their lives, expecting them eventually to become spiritual parents themselves.

Joe is a teacher at a public school in Indiana and a member of one of the small groups of a DOVE church there. He often volunteered to oversee extracurricular activities for the kids at his school and consequently built friendly relationships with many students and gained favor with the school's administration. Current and former students would frequently come over to his house to watch sporting events and talk. After the informal time, Joe would present a short Bible study. At first, most of the students left before the Bible study began, until one night a student decided to stay. He came back the next week and then started inviting his friends to stay. Week after week, more kids participated in the study and asked if they could receive Christ. At the end of the year, five young men Joe had been discipling were water baptized. Fifteen additional current and former students have since prayed to receive Christ. It is not unusual to see them and others filling up the couches at Joe's house on Sunday and Monday night for Bible study and prayer—and food, of course (these are high school students, after all!). Joe, even with help from his small group, has his hands full discipling these young men, but it is all worth it to see them growing in Jesus. These kids are being discipled so that eventually they can become spiritual parents themselves. And they are using the practical discipleship tool, called the *Biblical Foundation Series*, that we have developed to disciple new believers week after week in the basics of the Christian life. See appendix B for more details and insights on the 12-book *Biblical Foundation Series* discipleship tool that is now being used by thousands of churches throughout America.

Follow the Model of Jesus: Initiate, Build and Release

Spiritual parents will follow Jesus' model of initiating, building and releasing. Spiritual parents first take the initiative and get to know their spiritual son or daughter. This takes intentional effort! They could do things together they both enjoy—like fishing, scrapbooking, going to a sports game, or baking cookies.

When a solid foundation of relationship is laid, it's time to build. This can take on many shapes. If you are mentoring someone for ministry, take that person along to the hospital when you visit a sick church member. Allow him or her to see you serve as you use your gifts and knowledge. Be honest about mistakes you have made and challenges you have faced. Pray with your spiritual child regularly.

Finally, when you sense your son or daughter is ready, it's time to release them for on-the-job-training. As you observe your spiritual children testing what they've learned, evaluate them and give them feedback. This give-and-take allows them to apply and adapt to their own situations what they have seen you do. Give them assignments and help them set goals for developing their gifts. When spiritual parents are available to impart what they have learned, they are helping their sons and daughters reach their full potential as men and women of God.

In a spiritual parenting relationship, this takes place within an atmosphere of love and acceptance, without judgment or fear of rejection. It happens naturally by example and modeled behavior as spiritual parents initiate, build and release their family of spiritual children, imparting everything they have to give!

Non-negotiables of a Spiritual Parenting Relationship

Whatever shape your mentoring relationship takes, there are a few basics that apply. In my book *Authentic Spiritual Mentoring*, I (Larry) discuss the following non-negotiables in a spiritual parenting relationship.

Prayer
Prayer must be woven into the very fabric of the mentoring relationship. Praying for your spiritual son or daughter will wrap them in the Lord's protection and increase your sensitivity to their spiritual growth. Spiritual parenting cannot be just another item on your to-do list. Christians have enough meetings to attend and things to do already! Developing a spiritual mentoring relationship must be something the Lord imparts to you personally, and it must be birthed in prayer.

Hearing from God
Not only should spiritual parents diligently pray for their spiritual children, but they should also teach them to hear from

God for themselves and discern God's voice. The Lord has an enormous range of options for speaking to us. He may use the inner witness of the Holy Spirit, His Word, prayer, circumstances or other people. The Lord may speak to us in dreams, visions or even by His audible voice; however, don't expect God's audible voice to be the common way He will speak! God's voice often blends into a melodic harmony to which we have to tune in.

Accountability

Accountability is a way for us to check up on each other so that we stay on a safe path and remain responsible for our actions. Personal accountability is finding out from God what He wants us to do and then asking someone to help make sure we follow through on those behaviors. If a spiritual daughter wants to be held accountable by her spiritual mother for a certain area in her life that needs support, that doesn't mean the mother tells her what to do. The spiritual mother does not control the actions and decisions of her daughter. Instead, she forms a partnership with her protégé that results in good choices and personal growth. The daughter makes the final decision about what she will do in any given situation. Mentors point others to Jesus; in the end, each person is responsible for his or her own decisions.

Servanthood

Serving others must be the crux of the parenting relationship. Leading through service releases sons and daughters to be all they can be and empowers them to grow. When the mentoring relationship centers on servanthood, it gives people the freedom to use their own gifts and abilities.

Vulnerability

At the Last Supper, Jesus took off His outer garment and knelt down to wash the disciples' feet. Before an individual can serve others, he or she must take off his or her "outer garments." Here we can look at the outer garment as a metaphor for the "Sunday-best behavior" we must cast off to enter into real family relationships. Sometimes our outer garment is a cover-up to hide our vulnerabilities. We don't want others to see our weaknesses, so we keep our outer garments pulled around us, intact and stiff and getting in the way of real relationship. Opening up our lives to others is a complex and risky proposition. But honesty is both humbling and liberating. A "performance mentality" will go out the door when we share our real, uncloaked lives with others. Freed of our outer garments, we will no longer serve because we think it is required of us but because we love as God loved us.

As spiritual parents develop the kind of mentoring relationships their spiritual sons and daughters need, they are fulfilling the Acts 2 dynamic of a community of faith that exploded on the scene when the promised Holy Spirit empowered Jesus' followers to make disciples all over the world and reproduce themselves again and again.

Jesus' style of disciple-making has been all but lost in many parts of the Body of Christ. Yet the simple way that Jesus reproduced Himself in His followers should serve as the model for all believers. Now, here is our question for you as you face your future: Who will the "disciple Timothy" be in your life? Allow us to explain this question.

Paul really grasped the truth of disciple-making when he told Timothy, "You then, my son, be strong in the grace that is in Christ Jesus. And the things you have heard me say in the presence of many witnesses entrust to reliable men who will also be qualified to teach others" (2 Tim. 2:1-2, *NIV*). Paul exhorted Timothy, who was his disciple, to find another reproducing disciple who would disciple another.

We want to issue you a challenge that has the potential to change the world: Ask God for one reproducing disciple within the next few months. Just one! Sure, if you want to disciple more, go for it as God gives you the grace. But start with one, and encourage your "disciple" to disciple someone else next year. Then the pattern repeats as you each find another person to disciple who is also a reproducing disciple every year. In ten years, by just discipling one person each year who is also discipling one person, you will have contributed to the spiritual growth of more than 1,000 people!

After 20 years, at just one disciple per year, how many disciples do you think you will have influenced? Over one million! That's right, over 1,000,000 people in 20 years, at just one person each year. Do the math if you do not believe us. After 30 years, the number jumps to over one billion! No wonder the enemy has been hiding this truth from the Body of Christ and keeping us busy in activity—even religious activity. Now, there may be naysayers and doubters who are saying, "But we do not live in a perfect world. What if it breaks down?"

Our response is simple, "We will take a half million disciples if it breaks down."

Jesus said it like this: "The good seed stands for the sons of the kingdom" (Matt. 13:38, *NIV*). And the principles of discipleship are found in the parables of the sower (reproducing 30, 60 and 100 times) and in the parable of the mustard seed—a seed so small, with so much potential!

Our God is calling us to a new level of commitment to the dynamic truth of disciple-making. But most of us need tools to help us. Few school teachers teach without textbooks and resources to help them train their students one step at a time.

Here is one practical option for you. As I mentioned earlier, over the past 15 years I (Larry) released a 12-book biblical foundation series.[1] These 12 small books are practical tools filled with hundreds of Scriptures and real-life stories to help you disciple the next generation. All you need to do is take one chapter a week over the next year and discuss these vital foundational truths with your "Timothy." And guess what? When you help others with the basics of Christianity, *you* will also receive renewed insight from His Word to live victoriously above the struggles of daily life. Nearly 400,000 of these books have been used throughout the Body of Christ in our nation and the nations over the past few years. Both Antioch Community Church and DOVE Christian Fellowship International have used these simple discipleship books to bless thousands.

So, this is our one-person challenge to you as you approach this next season of your life. Find your "Timothy." Who is your reproducing young disciple, in the mold of 2 Timothy 2:2, going to be?

We love others by giving them our time as we help them grow in Christ. The Bible tells us, in Matthew 28:16-20, "Then the eleven disciples left for Galilee, going to the mountain where Jesus had told them to go. When they saw him, they worshiped him—but some of them doubted! Jesus came and told his disciples, 'I have been given all authority in heaven and on earth. Therefore, go and make disciples of all the nations, baptizing them in the name of the Father and the Son and the Holy Spirit. Teach these new disciples to obey all the commands I have given you. And be sure of this: I am with you always, even to the end of the age.'"

Jesus called everyone to make disciples, both the doubters and the worshipers. Regardless of how you feel today, He has called you! He gave His promise to us who are willing to make disciples, "And be sure of this: I am with you always, even to the end of the age."

So many we meet feel like this: "How could God ever use me? I don't know how to be a spiritual parent. I'm afraid. I don't know the Bible well enough. I need to get my life more together." If you feel this way, you have a lot of company.

Moses told the Lord he could not speak properly. Jeremiah told the Lord he was too young. Joshua was scared, and the Lord kept reassuring him that He would be with him just as He was with his "father" Moses. Gideon thought he was brought up in the wrong family for the Lord to use him. The list goes on and on.

Even the apostle Paul admitted to the Corinthian church that he had a deep sense of his own weakness that caused him to feel fearful and inadequate: "When I first came to you, dear brothers and sisters, I didn't use lofty words and impressive wisdom to tell you God's secret plan. For I decided that while I was with you I would forget everything except Jesus Christ, the one who was crucified. I came to you in weakness—timid and trembling" (1 Cor. 2:1-3). Nevertheless, Paul went on to declare that although his speech was not persuasive, the Holy Spirit's power was in his words (see v. 4). He said it another way in 2 Timothy 1:7: "For God has not given us a spirit of fear and timidity, but of power, love, and self-discipline."

Maybe you didn't go to seminary or Bible School, but however much you know is certainly more than the spiritual baby in Christ whom the Lord longs for you to mentor. Insecurities keep us paralyzed so that we never move beyond our comfort zones. However, if we trust and obey God, He will allow us to use our gifts and even increase them in His service. He will give us courage and resolution. God's love will always triumph over the fear of man.

There are still 2.1 billion people who have not heard the gospel and had a chance to respond to it. There are more than 10,000 people groups that do not have a life-giving Acts 2 gathering that is reproducing itself. When people discuss the best way to reach the whole world for Christ, the answer always seems clear to us: the Church. God wants to be known in all the earth. He wants to rightly distribute Himself so that all can hear and all can know. The way He has chosen to do that is through the Church.

We follow in the footsteps of thousands who have gone before us, but this is our time. It is our hour to see the coming of the Lord—to be a part of God's dream by answering His heart's cry.

Note
1. Larry Kreider, *Biblical Foundation Series* (Lititz, PA: House to House Publications, 1993).

LOVING A BROKEN
WORLD

Loving Those Separated from God

Stories of why we are so passionate about loving and reaching those who do not know Jesus

In 2005, I (Jimmy) flew into Kansas City and went to Thrifty Car Rental. As I finished my transaction with the lady behind the counter, I said, "I don't know if anyone has ever told you how much Jesus loves you. I know you're busy, but I'd love to leave you this little pamphlet that talks about God's love for you. When you get a chance, you can read it, and I know it will bless you." Not thinking much of it, I went on to the hotel and spent the next two days sharing at a local church.

On the second day, I was going to the church to teach in a training school. I was running late that morning, so I slipped quickly into McDonald's to grab a cup of coffee. As I ran in, the eyes of the girl at the counter got really big and round. She said excitedly, "Are you Jimmy, are you Jimmy?"

"Well, yes, I am," I said.

"Do you remember me?" she asked.

"I am so sorry, I don't," I responded.

She said, "This past summer you led me to Jesus in Colorado. You shared the gospel with me, and I gave my life to

Jesus, and I am involved in a church here in our city, and God's put my life together. I just wanted to let you know that it works! It works when you share with people; it changes their lives." I was stunned to hear how those little seeds produced such fruit.

After two days of teaching at the church, I returned my car to Thrifty and was sitting outside, waiting for the shuttle to take me to the airport. While I was waiting, a lady walked out and said, "Are you the guy that gave Susan that pamphlet about God's love a couple of days ago?"

I said, "Well, yes, I am."

She said, "Can I get a few more from you?"

As I was digging in my bag for more, I asked her, "Tell me what happened."

She said, "I felt that God wanted me to work here at Thrifty Car Rental, and I was frustrated because I wasn't seeing any fruit. The people I was loving and trying to share God's love with were not responsive, especially Susan. But yesterday Susan came over to me and said, 'A man just gave me a little pamphlet about God's love. I read it and I think it's very interesting.' As I looked at it and saw the clear presentation of the gospel, I told her this was exactly what God has for her and asked her if she would like to receive Jesus. We sat there in the back break room, and she prayed to receive Jesus. She came to church with me last night, and God is just rocking her world! Thank you for sharing the gospel, and now I want to go and do the same, knowing that it changes people's lives."

The simplicity of just sharing the gospel as we go through life is sometimes so powerful it is overwhelming. Our heart is to equip everyone to share their testimonies and to train them to be involved in this great adventure of seeing people come to Jesus. We train people to share their testimonies in one to three minutes, to walk through a simple presentation like "Steps to Peace with God" in order to clearly communicate the gospel, and to do relational evangelism by loving and caring for people in practical ways. We teach whole Lifegroups how to pray together, seek God together, and believe for friends and neighbors. We do corporate events where we share boldly on a weekly basis how people can come to know Jesus.

However God leads you to share it, this gospel is the power of God unto salvation, and when you see it at work, it allows you to see the love of God in a fresh way. It ignites joy in your heart like you've never experienced before, and it allows you to walk in that incredible adventure of the Kingdom that God has for you.

Our people consistently share the gospel and daily send me stories of people who have come to Jesus.

A few years ago, some of our college students went out spontaneously in evangelistic teams and attended parties around town. They would stand up in the middle of the crowd, get everyone's attention, and preach the gospel. After they shared, they made themselves available to anyone who wanted to talk.

At one of these parties, a guy named Kyle was listening. In his younger years, Kyle had been in church. But as a teenager and college student, he had fallen away from his faith. When our guys showed up at the party, Kyle was amazed that they were actually sharing the gospel and that they really believed what they were saying. His heart was drawn. Our guys stayed late into the night talking to Kyle. Before the night was over, he gave his life to Christ and poured his drugs down the toilet, choosing absolute surrender and freedom with the Lord.

The next Sunday, Kyle came to be baptized. He shared his testimony before the congregation, and then I baptized him.

Just as I was bringing him up out of the water, a man in the back row stood up and shouted over hundreds of people, "My son was dead, but now he is alive!" Kyle's father, who had also not been to church in a long while, had slipped into the back of the church. Seeing the power and grace of God, he couldn't help but stand up and shout. The place erupted with rejoicing as we celebrated the power of new life. "In the same way, I tell you, there is joy in the presence of the angels of God over one sinner who repents" (Luke 15:10, *NASB*).

It Takes Intentional Effort

Two thousand years ago, a small group of ordinary people proclaimed the good news of Jesus Christ and began a movement that changed the world. Imagine what can happen if you, empowered by the Holy Spirit, learn to respond to the Great Commission and begin to love people into the kingdom of God! You can do it, you know. You are a representative of Jesus. As you model authentic Christianity in word and deed, your efforts to reach people for Jesus will draw them to Him. Evangelism certainly takes intentional effort. It doesn't just happen that authentic Christian disciples—disciples grounded, shaped and transformed by the grace of Jesus Christ—are produced.

Amy is a young woman from Indianapolis Christian Fellowship, one of the DOVE churches in Indiana. For several months, Amy had been talking with Jim, a fellow engineer at work, about the Lord. He would share struggles he was having with his family, opening the door for her to share Jesus with him.

One day, Amy could tell something was really troubling Jim. He told her that his father, Jim Sr., was dying, and he talked about how difficult it was on the entire family. In fact, his father had been asking about God lately. He was afraid to die.

Immediately, Amy began to pray. "Oh Father, give me the wisdom to know what to do!" Amy's small group's desire was to reach out to the people they related to on a daily basis. Amy quickly realized this was a wide open door for her small group to pray. From her computer, she emailed everyone in her group, asking them to start praying that the Lord would give her wisdom about how to reach this man and his family.

The group was extremely supportive. Within one hour, Amy received two emails from members who were praying for her. One of the members, Julie, knew Jim personally because she used to work with him. She offered to go with Amy to pray for Jim's father and was excited at the opportunity to share Jesus with someone who desperately needed hope.

At work the next day, Amy asked Jim if she could pray with his father. He was open to the idea, so that night Amy and Julie drove to Jim Sr.'s house.

When they arrived, Jim Sr. and his wife, Sandy, were there. They talked for a while, getting to know one another, and then the women asked their hosts what they would like prayer for. Jim Sr. immediately acknowledged that he was afraid to die. Amy and Julie shared the concepts of salvation and eternal life with him, gave him a Bible, and walked him through the "Romans Road"—a series of verses found in Romans that clearly outlines the salvation message.

After discussing these verses, they had the privilege of leading Jim Sr. to receive Jesus as his personal Lord and Savior! Amy recalls, "At work the next day, Jim thanked me for praying with his parents. I told him it was our pleasure, meanwhile thinking to myself, 'You're next!' I mentioned that our small group had offered to bring over dinner for his family or help them with other daily chores. He was amazed that people who didn't even know him would offer to help his family."

True to their word, Amy's group made dinner and took it to Jim Sr. and Sandy's house. The next day at work, Jim Jr. couldn't stop thanking Amy for the dinner. Later that day, he asked her for directions so he could bring his family to her group. The small group is currently praying for this family. Though Amy is the one with the closest relationship with the family, the group members all play a role—especially one of prayer. It is a way they can intentionally work together to reach the lost!

Believers from The Fireplace, one of the DOVE churches in Pennsylvania, had been knocking on every door in their town for much of the summer because they had a genuine burden for the lost people in their community. They had also been meeting in the local park for church services in an effort to get out of their building and their comfort zone. They were determined to take the kingdom of God to people. Although going door to door to share the gospel was their least favorite way to evangelize, they realized that evangelism was not happening in their church, so they had to take an intentional step forward.

Before they went, they made sure everyone was trained to give a short presentation of the gospel. Initially, they received a wide array of responses from their door-to-door efforts. Some were positive, but many of the people they encountered were cold to the gospel message or too busy to listen.

One Sunday, during a time of prayer in the park, God gave the pastor an impression that there was a woman waiting for them—waiting to hear the gospel. They worshiped for a short time, and then split up into small groups and went out into the town. One group, after going door to door and not finding anyone at home, was getting discouraged. Finally, a man opened the door to his house and told them he did not have time to hear what they had to say. They turned to go, and as they walked across the lawn, the man's wife came running after them in her bathrobe. "Please come back another time to talk about Jesus," she said.

Then things started picking up. The group went to the next house, and a woman named Beth came to the door and invited them in. She began to weep when they told her why they had come. Beth said she had bought a Bible six years ago and had been seeking God ever since. Needless to say, she accepted the Lord immediately with tears of joy!

All of the small groups went back to the park where they were meeting for the church service. At the park, a young man, Brian, came to Christ and wanted to be baptized. During lunch, a young girl and her friend accepted Jesus as well. The Lord gave incredible joy to the believers at The Fireplace that day as people gave their lives to Jesus.

Early on, we began asking God for power evangelism—we wanted people to see the power of God and be saved. So we decided to coordinate a Saturday morning evangelistic outreach group that would meet every Saturday from nine to noon. One Saturday morning, I (Jimmy) prayed for one of the students in our training school, and the power of God fell so heavily on him that I felt heat like fire in my hands. This young man then went out with his ministry partner for the day to share the gospel door to door. One family invited them in and gathered around to hear the good news preached. That afternoon, the whole family came to Christ.

It was during those Saturday morning outreaches that the Lord began to teach us how He divinely leads us if we ask Him. I remember walking through a neighborhood asking the Lord whom I should talk to. There were several people out in their yards, so my question was, "Lord, which one?" I felt the Spirit direct me very strongly to a certain lady named Sarah. As I approached her, I asked the Lord what I should say to her.

"Do you know Jesus?" I asked Sarah.

"No, I don't," she replied. "But I just got out of the hospital, and while I was there, I had a dream of falling into a black hole. I could tell that I was falling away from a light, and I was screaming out to that light. Can you tell me what that light is?"

Blown away by what I was hearing, I gladly explained to her that the light was Jesus. He had spared her life so that I could come and share His gospel with her so that she could be saved. Sarah gave her heart to the Lord that day. Her husband, Michael, eventually gave his life to the Lord as well, and Laura and I were able to spend time discipling them as a couple.

Because I want to be sowing the gospel daily, I often leave the "Steps to Peace with God" tracts in various places. One time I was in Phoenix, Arizona, and had gone to the restroom and left a tract on top of the toilet roll. Then I went out into the crowded restaurant, asking God this question: "Spirit of God, is there someone You are highlighting that needs to know You today?"

God directed me to a young man in his mid-20s. I went over to him and said, "This may sound crazy, but I really felt like God told me to come over and to just tell you that He loves you and He cares about you." The guy looked stunned—shocked!

He said, "You won't believe what just happened. I was in the bathroom and I picked up this little pamphlet called 'Steps to Peace with God.' As I read it, my heart was pounding."

I asked him to tell me his story. He said, "When I was younger, my dad was a pastor in a church. He committed adultery and left my mom. I never talked to him again. I've resisted God and the people of God for years. I'm having a tough time right now, and I have just been saying, 'God, are You real? Are You out there? Do You know where I live?' and then this happened today, and now here you are."

I said, "God not only knows who you are but He knows how to love you and how to care for you. Today is the day of grace for you."

As I prayed over him, this young man wept and gave his life to Jesus. I kept up with him for the next three or four months and found out that he got established in a church and began to walk with Jesus.

On one occasion, we were on a mission trip to England with one of our training schools. While sharing the gospel, we encountered an atheist who had a broken leg; the break was a week old. This man mocked us openly, but the students just offered to pray for him. After they prayed, he left us to go to a doctor's appointment. At the doctor's office, he learned that his leg was healed! He called the church that sponsored the training school, told the elders what had happened, and gave his life to Christ that day.

This man was the principal at a local school. He went to work and testified to more than 300 students that God had healed him supernaturally. Many of the students from his school came to Christ as well. The following Sunday, the principal came to church to testify about God's goodness, and through this miracle, the church rejoiced and grew.

On another occasion, as we went from house to house, a lady answered when we knocked on her door. We offered to pray with her and share our testimony, but she became irate, saying, "Don't tell me that Jesus loves me or cares! God doesn't care about me!"

I asked, "Why do you think that?"

"Look at my son," she said. A little six- or seven-year-old boy appeared. "He has mental problems and was just diagnosed with colon cancer."

Our hearts broke with her. We told her that we understood her pain and that we wanted to pray that God would heal her child. Softened by the compassion we showed for her son, she let us lay hands on him and pray. What a delightful little boy he was, smiling and hugging us while we prayed over him.

This was the next-to-last day before we left England. The boy was having surgery the following morning, and we went to visit him in the hospital to see how he was doing. When we arrived, the mother had this incredible look of excitement and shock on her face. "What happened?" we asked.

She said that when the doctors ran one last X-ray before doing the surgery, they found that the cancer was gone. She held up both of the X-rays and said, "The cancer is gone. God has healed my son." As we hugged her and cried together, we rejoiced over a God who sees the pain and need in people's hearts and shows up in miraculous ways.

During one of our services while we were in Scotland, we were waiting on the Lord, asking Him where we should go that day. God gave me a picture of a horseshoe and a bar. When I asked one of the Scottish men if there was a place like that nearby, he directed me to a pub on High Street.

I followed the man's directions, found the place, and walked in. "Hey, I want to share with you guys about how much God loves you," I said to the entire crowd. No one seemed interested at first, but I went ahead and shared the gospel anyway. When I was finished, one guy waved me over. We went to a side booth, and he told me his story: The night before, he had tried to kill himself. Just as he had taken a knife to his throat, an invisible hand had stopped him and caused him to crumple to his knees. His experience made him think that God existed, but he didn't know how he could know God.

When he finished his story, I gladly shared the gospel with him and led him to Christ. His girlfriend eventually came to Christ as well, and they both got involved in the church.

Those summer outreaches continued to show us that God was at work all over the world, and He wanted us to join Him.

The Fruit of Reaching Out Beyond Our Borders

After the summer during which God changed my life as a young man, I (Jimmy) returned to college, and my buddy Kyle and I went on a bike ride. So many great things were going on that I asked him, "Hey, man, what do we do with all of this that is happening in our lives?"

He said, "Have you ever heard of missions?"

"No," I responded.

"Missions is where you go tell people about Jesus in other nations," he explained.

"Wow, it sounds great to me. Do you know anybody that knows anything about it?"

"I don't know," he said. "But why don't we pray and ask God to show us?"

The next morning, Kyle and I went to Sunday School at Highland Baptist Church with some friends. As we broke up into classes, someone said that there was a missionary from Thailand who was going to talk about God's call to missions. Kyle and I looked at each other and said, "Let's go."

The missionary spoke from Matthew 28:19-20 about God's call to the Church to share Jesus with the nations. Well, having just learned how to apply the words of Jesus that I had read in Matthew that summer, I was impressed with this missionary's message and life. I wanted to encourage him that he was doing a great job of preaching exactly what the Bible said.

After his talk, Kyle and I, along with our friends Bill and Susan, went to affirm him. I am sure I came across as naïve and maybe even ignorant as I told him what a great job he was doing, but he was very gracious to us. He explained that he had a friend in Papua New Guinea who looks for lost tribes who have never heard the gospel. "He would love to have students join him next summer if you guys are interested."

Immediately we said, "Yes, that would be great!" Bill, Susan and I went to lunch and dreamed about the adventure. Over the next few months, we saw God move powerfully as we prepared to go and eventually found ourselves in the jungles of New Guinea in the summer of 1985. This was my first experience of reaching out to those who had never heard of Jesus.

I have met some amazing missionaries in my day, but I will never forget the first one I was privileged to work with in New Guinea: David Sitton. He was like an Indiana Jones for Jesus, trekking through the mountains to share the gospel at any cost.

Our first journey into the jungle with David to reach lost tribes was quite eventful. We took the four-wheel-drive truck as far as it would go along the jungle roads and then hiked the rest of the way to the river. There, we met local Papuans straight from the pages of *National Geographic*—bones through their noses, loincloths, the whole works. These men were our guides to take us upriver to a village that had not yet heard the gospel.

As we sat in our handmade dugout canoes and went up the Sepik River, I realized what we had done. I thought to myself, "You're stupid—you are crazy. What in the world have you gotten into? You are going to die out here in the middle of the jungle." As we went along the tributaries, the rain started falling and darkness set in. As I stared into the red eyes of the crocodiles swimming around us, making sure to keep my hands inside the boat, I became keenly aware of our need for God. This was not all fun and games; the adventure had become reality, and it was serious. We were going to have to find God on another level.

When we docked, the villagers extended a plank to get us ashore. Bill and I carried a generator across, but when I reached the top, the plank broke in half and all six-feet-two-inches and 230 pounds of Bill fell into the crocodile-infested river. I had never seen anyone walk on water, nor have I since. But within seconds, Bill was out of the water and running past me on the bank!

As we pitched our tents that night to go to bed, we wondered if this venture was worth the trouble. The next morning though, we found out that it was. Because local folklore taught the villagers of a creator god and a great flood, we started our presentation of truth with a slide show about creation and the flood. We then explained that the God they had been trying to appease for years was not a God of terror but one of love. That first morning in the village, we saw 19 people give their hearts to the Lord. Over the ensuing days, many of the villagers did so as well.

The night before we left this area, a man sent for us. Suffering from cancer, he had laid on his mat for two months unable to get up. He explained that he wanted God either to heal him or to end his misery and let him die. We shared the gospel with him, and he gladly accepted Christ as his Savior. Then, we prayed for his healing but did not see any immediate result. The next morning, as we were packing up to leave, one of the villagers ran to us and said, "The old man is up! The old man is up! He is fixing breakfast for you. He has been healed."

David took us on many adventures in the mountains of New Guinea. Those were exciting and terrifying days, as we took the gospel to places it had never before been proclaimed. I remember one particular journey where we had been dropped off on a grass airstrip with the pilot's assurance that he would return within a week. What a comforting promise to a group of missionaries looking for the last cannibal tribes!

God was so faithful during those days. He protected us from harm and disease. He provided through the kindness of locals. He guided our steps and strengthened us when we were at the end of ourselves. Most amazingly, He allowed us to step into the adventure of sharing the gospel with those living in the farthest reaches of the world.

The bottom line is that we should always want to be a church with a mission. A church with a mission has people who are driven by the purposes of Jesus, whether we are at home or in a foreign culture. Focusing energy, love and attention on our neighbors is our heart's investment in what God has placed before us. Even as we aggressively send people around the world, we desire first to go to our neighbors.

8

Reaching Out in Everyday Life

How we can each experience a return to loving and reaching the lost in authentic ways

Brent is a member of one of the DOVE churches in Canada. Brent's wife became a Christian a couple of years before Brent's spiritual awakening. While anxious to share her faith with her husband, she made a conscious effort not to be "in his face" about it. Her new church friends also made Brent feel comfortable and unthreatened. They didn't make Brent feel like a heathen if he drank a beer at a gathering or let a swear word slip out around them. They did not look to create an opportunity to pitch the gospel to him at every turn.

The stuffy, holier-than-thou attitude Brent thought was a part of the born-again Christian community clearly was absent. Brent says, "Eventually, the Holy Spirit and the Word showed me the error of my ways and helped me correct them, but at the time I wouldn't have tolerated anyone else's input. My time is too precious to commit to something that is threatening or uncomfortable, regardless of the cause. My wife's church made me feel like I was being offered friendship for the sake of friendship. No strings attached, no ulterior motives. Because of these friendships, I began tearing down my walls instead of building them up."

For 36 years, no one had been able to convince Brent of the reality of heaven or of the wrath of God. But the love and patience of a caring community softened his heart and led him to become one of God's children.

Dorothy, a DOVE church member from Pennsylvania, realized she must increase relationships with people for whom her small group had been praying. This group had a Spanish-speaking leader, so the members knew from the start that God had placed them near the mushroom farms of Reading, Pennsylvania, for a specific reason—to cultivate relationships and friendships with the Mexican migrant workers. Dorothy was hesitant about visiting the farm workers at first because she spoke only English. How could she show her love to them without even basic verbal communication?

On her first visit, Dorothy met Bernardo while he was working in his garden. Despite the language barrier, they had an instant rapport as she shared her love of gardening by pointing out different seedlings and identifying them with Bernardo. Then Dorothy and others shared with a larger group of workers how God cared about their tears and loneliness in a strange place. The love God poured out that day was tangible. Dorothy and her husband had so much fun, they couldn't wait to go back.

Since that first contact, Dorothy and the other small-group members have made many friends at the farms. Pizza parties, Bible studies and English classes are all a part of their regular activities with the workers. Seven men have prayed to receive Christ and are being discipled by members of the DOVE group.

Jesus knew how to have an impact on people while eating with them or through other relational activities. We can naturally get involved in pre-Christians' lives by looking for opportunities to share non-religious experiences with them based on common interests. Such activities can include sports, garden clubs, backyard barbecues, lunch, coffee breaks, helping a neighbor with a project like building a fence, planting a garden, and a host of other opportunities. Developing friendships with our neighbors or those in the workplace starts with being genuinely friendly. You have to show an interest in people's stories and listen to them before they will hear what you have to say. When people feel heard and understood, they will begin to trust you enough to consider your perspective. It all starts with becoming a friend.

A study was conducted with more than 14,000 lay people who were asked the question: "What or who was responsible for you coming to Christ and your church?" Out of the categories of "special need, walk-in, pastor, visitation, Sunday School, evangelistic crusade, church program, and friend/relative," 75 to 90 percent came to Christ through a friend or relative. The conclusion is clear. The great majority of people can point to a friend or relative as the primary reason for why they are in Christ and in their church.[1]

Becoming Friends: The *Oikos* Principle

Oikos is the Greek word for "household" or "house of people." Your *oikos* is that group of people with whom you relate on a regular basis. Every believer should apply the *oikos* principle to their lives as a way of infiltrating their spheres of influence with the gospel of Jesus Christ as they reach out beyond themselves.

Acts 10:2 speaks of Cornelius and all of his family (*oikos*). He and all his family were devout and God-fearing; he gave generously to those in need and prayed to God regularly. Later in the chapter, we read that "Cornelius was waiting for [Peter] and had called together his relatives and close friends [his *oikos*]" (Acts 10:24).

Another instance of *oikos* occurs when Paul and Silas were in prison. In the midst of an earthquake, the jailer became receptive to the gospel. He invited his household to listen to Paul's message, and they were all made acceptable to God through faith in Christ. This group of people was his *oikos*.

The *oikos* principle is a strategy of using our existing relationships to evangelize and to make disciples. Wendy, a teenager from one of the DOVE churches, befriended Susi, an atheist German exchange student at her school. She invited Susi along to her small group, and over the next several months, Susi soaked in God's Word and asked many challenging questions of her new-found friends. It was an exciting day for the entire group when Susi announced she had made Jesus the Lord of her life and wanted to be baptized. Susi was a natural part of Wendy's *oikos*.

Groups of people who are a part of your *oikos* include the following:

- *Family and relatives.* Your Uncle Jack and Aunt Judy and cousin Ted are all part of your oikos, even if they live far away. If you maintain regular contact with them, they are part of your oikos.

- *Those who have common interests with you.* Those who play tennis with you are part of your *oikos*. Anyone with whom you share a common interest—such as computers, video games, sports, sewing, playing basketball, playing the guitar—these people are part of your *oikos*.

- *Those who live in the same geographical location as you.* Your neighbors are part of your *oikos*.

- *Those who share your vocation.* Those with whom you work—your fellow employees—are part of your *oikos*. If you are a construction worker, your *oikos* includes other construction workers. If you are a doctor, other medical professionals that you relate with would be included in your *oikos*.

- *Others with whom you have regular contact.* These people may include your dentist, family doctor, mechanic, hairdresser, salespeople or school officials. People in your *oikos* group will tend to be receptive to the gospel (in God's timing) because they trust you—you have built a relationship with them. Sometimes a Christian may discover that his or her *oikos* includes only other believers. When this is the case, steps need to be taken to develop new circles of relationships. A believer might join a soccer team, neighborhood organization or other community group to widen his or her *oikos*. More than 30 years ago, when my wife, LaVerne, and I (Larry) and a group of young people began to play baseball, basketball and other sports with youth in our local community, we built relationships with them, and they became a part of our *oikos*. Because we established friendships with them on their turf, we could readily discuss the good news of Jesus. Our *oikos* is part of God's strategy to reach the world.

One day, Jesus ministered to a man who was demon possessed. After he was delivered, the man begged Jesus for permission to

The 3 Loves

follow Him. However, Jesus said, " 'No, go back to your family, and tell them everything God has done for you.' So he went all through the town proclaiming the great things Jesus had done for him" (Luke 8:39).

Jesus sent this man home to his *oikos*! When Levi invited Jesus to his home for dinner, he also invited his *oikos* members (see Luke 5:27-32). Zacchaeus had Jesus come to his home, and his whole household accepted Christ. This was his *oikos* (see Luke 19:1-10). Andrew asked Simon to come and get to know Jesus. Simon was a member of Andrew's *oikos* (see John 1:40-42). Philip asked Nathanael to come and get to know Jesus. Nathanael was part of Philip's *oikos* (see John 1:44-45).

We have many everyday *oikos* opportunities. Ryan served as a small-group leader at a DOVE church until he and his family moved to another state, where they continued to be involved in small-group ministry. Ryan relates this story from a few years back—he was at the drive-in movies when God used him:

> It was just another Saturday night when my wife and I took my young cousin to a Disney movie at the drive-in. We parked our very used Toyota with Jesus stickers plastered all over the back window, and I stepped out of the car to go to the snack bar. A guy named Jon stopped me and asked if I was a Christian, and then proceeded to tell me his story of a life lived in disobedience to God. I told him how Jesus changed my life and that before I knew God, I was hurting and longing for real purpose. I explained how I had tried to find fulfillment in sports and later had joined the U.S. Marine Corps in hopes that being successful there would bring me a sense of accomplishment. That night, Jon knelt right beside

that snack bar at the drive-in and made Jesus the Lord of his life.

The next week, my wife and I, with my little cousin, returned to the drive-in and parked the car. This time, before I could even get out of the car, a woman I had never seen before came to the car and asked if I was the person who had prayed with Jon. She asked me to come to her car to meet Jon's mom [notice the expanding *oikos*!]. This precious lady, who had been an alcoholic for years, asked Jesus into her life that night and was set free!

Ryan took the time to hear Jon's story, paving the way for Jon to hear from God. Jon passed on what he learned to his mother who desperately needed Jesus, and the *oikos* expanded.

Many times, God calls us to reach out from that place of influence that we have in living our normal lives in our community. For Laura and me (Jimmy), one of our outlets became recreational sports clubs. Our kids all enjoyed sports, and one of those sports was soccer. As I coached on the soccer team, I tried to live with integrity and encouragement—to live out values before the kids and before their parents, whether they were believers or unbelievers, in a way that would create conversations that would give people an opportunity to respond to the gospel. Jake was one of the boys I coached for a couple of years. His dad, Rick, would come to the practices and games and was always very vocal. Many times, Rick was so vocal that he was asked to leave the field by the officials. In fact, he had such a problem of rage that he was threatened to be banned from the games forever.

One day, Rick saw me on TV being interviewed about our situation in Afghanistan. The next time he saw me, he came up to me and said, "You [blankety-blank]! I can't believe you're a blanking pastor! Why didn't you tell me?"

You see, I had loved Rick. I let him share his struggles and his pain, and I simply prayed for him but never communicated that I was a pastor because I wanted him to know that I was just a normal guy who loves Jesus, and I wanted to help him. As he and I began to talk about his rage and challenges in life, he communicated a deep need to be free. Rick and I got together and, first and foremost, I explained to him that the only way to change was through a relationship with Jesus Christ. If he would give his life to Christ, that would begin a process of setting him free. Rick and I prayed that day in my office, and he gave his life to Jesus. Five minutes later, I began to take him through a booklet called "Steps to Freedom in Christ" by Neil Anderson. Each of those steps helps to clean the house from the past, so that you can move forward with your life.

During those days, Rick experienced forgiveness, he experienced healing and restoration, and he began a journey of restoring his family. He invited his wife, Terri, to meet with me; she then also gave her life to Jesus. Slowly but surely, each of their children gave their lives to Jesus. Rick, Terri and two of their children were all baptized on the same day, proclaiming that Jesus is Lord.

Rick and Terri remain with us today. They are involved in leading small groups and helping people get closer to Jesus, even as they continue to journey themselves towards Christlikeness. What's always fun is that whenever I preach, Rick is the first guy to come up to me and tell me, "That's exactly what I needed." He calls me almost every week and leaves a message on my phone. Rick has become my number one encourager. It's amazing what God can do when we just intentionally keep our eyes open for every opportunity, even at our kids' sporting events, to share about Him. God's desire is to change the world, and that is done one life at a time, in one arena of society at a time, for His glory.

Doing What Jesus Would

Kurt heard a loud clanging at the gate in his home in Afghanistan. Instinctively, he knew something was wrong. By the time he got to the door, his Afghan friend, Andrew (his alias name), had already opened the gate.

Just past Andrew stood a group of men wearing black turbans, with eyeliner to highlight the fierceness of their gazes. One man had a curved sword pulled out. Two others held rods that looked like barbed wire covered with leather.

"Allah is not pleased, Andrew," they said. "You did not come to pre-dawn prayers at the mosque. We will subject you to the punishment. First, we will beat you with these rods, and then we will shave your head and take you to the prison run by the religious police for 13 days of forced prayer and teaching at the feet of the mullah. Then you will know how to obey Allah."

At that point, they saw Kurt, though at first they didn't know he was a foreigner because he wore the local clothing. "Sirs," Kurt said in their language, "Andrew was my guest last night. He was making me tea this morning. He is my friend. It is my fault that he didn't go to the mosque." Kurt stretched his arms out and went on to say, "If you are going to beat anyone, here, I am the one."

The two men dropped their rods, the other man put his sword back in its sheath, and all three lowered their heads and walked away. The Taliban had walked away.

Andrew shut the gate, looked at Kurt with wide eyes, and said, "Why did you step into our darkness? Why did you offer to take my beating? You are a guest in this country. You didn't need to do that."

Kurt responded in simple humility, "Andrew, Jesus Christ was willing to take the beating and punishment that I deserved, that I might be set free. I am only doing what was done for me."

Our Mission, Should We Choose to Accept It

Loving others and bringing them to Jesus is our mission on earth, and this mission we are a part of is worth our lives. Jesus is worthy of our very lives. Whatever the outcome of our journey of faith, we will come out fine if we love and serve Him by sharing the good news and laying down our lives for the people He has called us to.

When individuals in small groups and churches challenge one another to reach beyond themselves to make disciples, they will discover that God will give them many creative opportunities. Even if no one immediately comes to Christ through these opportunities, there is a spiritual dynamic released in the group that keeps our focus on the harvest fields instead of on ourselves. As we continue to sow, we will eventually reap.

There are many different creative approaches to reaching pre-Christians and making disciples. I (Larry) was once part of a small group in our church that printed up an attractive flyer with a big photo of our smiling group. One summer we canvassed our neighborhood by handing out the flyer, along with a small houseplant, to those who were newcomers to the community. We welcomed the new families to the neighborhood and invited them to our small group at the same time.

Some youth small groups have used clowning as a regular outreach ministry for their groups. Dressed as clowns, these young people go to parks, visit the elderly, and generally spread cheer and the good news of Jesus wherever they go as they hand out balloons and perform short skits.

Picnic evangelism is an informal way to reach family and friends with the message that God loves us and sent His Son so we can find forgiveness and new life through Him. Take the initiative to invite friends and relatives who have not made a decision to follow Christ to a picnic including free food, games and entertainment. Sharing Christ at picnics is a big hit with some DOVE Kenya small groups in Nairobi; given the area's warm climate, picnics are possible throughout most of the year. Through the outreach of these family-oriented picnics, relationships are built and people come to faith in Christ.

I wear contact lenses. A few years ago, my optometrist asked me if I was willing to try mono-vision. "What is mono-vision?" I asked. He explained that I would wear two completely different contacts, one to read and one to see at a distance, and I would then be able to see both near and far at practically the same time. Within a split second, my brain would respond to my two different contact lenses.

I tried it and loved it. Then one day it really hit me: God has called us as believers in Jesus to have spiritual mono-vision. We need to find ways to pray and reach those with whom we rub shoulders each day in our communities. But we also need to ask the Lord to connect us with those in other parts of the world who need Jesus. Joining a short-term mission team can change your life and perspective forever. Get your passport! Then you will be ready when the Lord opens the door for you to share the love of Jesus in another part of the world.

With the social networks of Facebook, Twitter, MySpace—the list goes on and on—experiencing spiritual mono-vision is much easier today than it was ten years ago. Relationships are built and maintained worldwide via cyberspace. Loving Jesus, loving His people, and loving those who need Jesus—this is what life is all about!

Note
1. Win and Charles Arn, *The Master's Plan for Making Disciples* (Pasadena, CA: Church Growth Press, 1982), p. 43.

IGNITING THE
PASSION

The Church Changes the World

Why we need to get back to where it all began

Where do we go from here? It all started in the New Testament, and it was so simple. The believers loved Jesus, loved each other and sincerely loved those who had not yet experienced Jesus' love and forgiveness. A spiritual fire and passion was ignited that changed the world! And these believers were genuine followers of Jesus, not just religious.

The Church is not a building, but a group of people. Acts 2:42-47 captures the heartbeat and the essence of the Church. When I talk to our people about the power of the Church to change the world, I shout out, "Church," and they shout back, "Acts 2:42-47." It is this expression of the kingdom of God through the Church that changes the world.

Several years ago, Bill Gates and his peers stated that they had a goal to have the whole world online by 2010. As Bill Gates and others researched this goal, they realized that there were one billion people nearing starvation in the world. There were one billion people in the world who didn't have their basic needs met. They knew where everyone in the world was, but the basic needs of these people were not being met. Many times, we say that God does not care. It is not that God does not care; the problem is that man does not rightly share God's love, which holds the answer to the world's problems. It is a distribution problem.

When I (Jimmy) was in Papua New Guinea, after traveling through the jungle for days somebody in one of the remote villages came up to me and gave me a Coke. I realized that the "Coke" man had beaten Christians to the outer reaches of the earth. Surely this grieves the heart of God! His desire is for us to go and share the gospel and to distribute His Kingdom. But we can't just do it alone; we need to do it as a people gathered into Acts 2 communities. When you think about discipleship, think about doing it together with a community of people and reproducing it all over the world.

Recently, tons of medicine intended to save the lives of Afghan children suffering from dysentery got stuck in customs in Pakistan because of bribes and red tape. These essential medicines couldn't get through. The provision was there, but something blocked the way. The same happens to us. It breaks the heart of God when something in us blocks the distribution of His love in all the earth. The Church is the answer to the world. Not the building, not the institution, but the gathered people of God—living Acts 2 communities. It says in Acts 2:47, "And the Lord was adding to their number day by day those who were being saved" (*NASB*).

In Ephesians 3:9-11, Paul says that the Church is the "administration" of the gospel. This word means that believers are the means of distribution of this "good news" message. The glory of God will cover the earth as the waters cover the seas, not just by individuals expressing the glory of God but instead because the gathered people of God multiply out His life in various regions of the world so that people can see Jesus, not only personally but through community.

I've realized from years of traveling around the world, and from Scripture itself, that God's desire is that all have the opportunity to hear the gospel. Matthew 24:14 says, "This gospel of the kingdom shall be preached in the whole world as a testimony to all the nations, and then the end will come" (*NASB*). Jesus will come when He sees fit, but one thing I know for sure is that He will come when His people are obedient to preach the gospel in all the earth.

A young Chinese man, whom we call Larry, came to Irkutsk, Russia, to complete a language program. He met Christ through our church plant in that city, joined a Lifegroup, and was discipled. Larry eventually became a Lifegroup leader and learned how to invest in others and to reproduce the life of Jesus. After Larry had been with the church in Irkutsk for about a year and a half, his visa expired, and he had to return to China. Our team prayed for Larry and sent him out, hoping to keep in touch.

Two years passed without any contact from Larry. Michael, one of the leaders in Irkutsk, and his wife, Linda (an American team member), had a heart for China. God gave them a desire to go to Larry's city to plant a church.

When they visited, they found Larry and asked him, "Are you still following Jesus?"

Larry looked at them strangely as if to say, *Well, of course I'm still following Jesus.*

They went on to ask him, "Have you found the underground church or other people to worship with?"

Larry responded, "All I did when I got here was what you told me to do. I gathered my friends and told them about my faith and what God was doing. Many of them came to Christ, and we began to meet in my home to talk about growing together in Jesus. They began reaching out and starting their own groups. Now we have about 120 people meeting in different homes in the city."

Michael and Linda spent the next two years with Larry and saw the group grow to 500. God's plan is always to capture people's hearts, allowing them to invest in community and learn to reproduce that community wherever they go. I believe we have stepped into what Jesus proclaimed when He said, "I will build My church; and the gates of Hades will not overpower it" (Matt. 16:18, *NASB*). God is looking for anybody to join His work of reproducing His life through the Church for His glory.

Reaching the Whole Person

Our God always meets us right where we are. Charles and Rose Wanyama are pastors of a DOVE church in Kibera (near Nairobi, Kenya), arguably the world's largest slum. In reaching out to the poorest of the poor, Rose wanted to do something that would meet not only spiritual but also physical and practical needs. She opened Joysprings School out of a vision for a school that would minister to families and the community. "At the school where I had been teaching, I was not allowed to 'waste time' talking to parents," she explained. So with the money from her final paycheck, she opened her own one-room school.

The first day, she had four students; the second day, she had 11. "Every morning, we prayed together. I would ask the children, 'What do you need from God?' They prayed for food, school clothes, textbooks and desks."

Rose carefully divided her few pencils into three pieces, so each child could have something to write with. "When I had spare food in my house, I would bring porridge (oatmeal) for the school children. It's hard to teach children who are hungry."

"We became known in the community for high academic standards," Rose explains. But even more notable was her willingness to educate children who were too impoverished to pay. "Without education, kids can't find their way out of the slums. Although there was no profit for me, the satisfaction was there. I was reaching kids and their parents."

In 2002, two years after the school was founded, a local seamstress donated 20 school uniforms to Joysprings. "The children saw their prayers answered, and they kept on praying." That same year, Rose received a micro-loan from a church donor and immediately bought maize and beans to start a lunch program. The number of students doubled from 30 to 60 students, and the children could count on at least one healthy meal each day.

"Our vision is to bring up healthy children, and children of character. Kibera is a place of crime and prostitution; we teach them about responsibility, leadership, faithfulness and right living." The discipleship is crucial, because most of these children basically raise themselves. Rose, her husband, Charles, and their staff are everything to many of these kids—parents, pastors and counselors. "When we close school for holidays, the children do not want to stay at home. There is no one at home, and no food. When they are at home, they have to fetch water and wash their clothes.

"A donor sent money to help us buy space for the school, and we purchased one quarter of a row house." The building housed 20 one-room units, and Rose eventually bought the second section of the building.

By 2010, the school had more than 400 students in 10 classrooms with 18 staff members. World Food Programme supplies school lunches, and the students have basic materials and school clothes. Their prayers are being answered.

Rose concludes, "This school is making an impact." Rose's greatest satisfaction comes from the children. They have a deep sense of ownership, pride and belonging in the school. Joysprings education is a ladder for these kids to climb out of a life of poverty in the slums. The church is making an impact in this community by showing God's love in practical ways. Charles and Rose are seeing the largest slum in the world being transformed by the power and love of Jesus, one person at a time.

Jackie and Bret's Story

Jackie was a freshman college student in love with Jesus. She was tender and compassionate and shared Christ boldly. Though her love for Jesus was genuine, she struggled with an eating disorder. This bondage led to her dropping out of school after her third year. After counsel and help, she returned to school, still loving Jesus.

Bret had suffered a sports injury in high school that caused him migraine headaches almost daily and severe pain 24 hours a day. The pain was so intense that he could hardly focus to study. Doctors had tried everything, but the ligaments had been so damaged that there was nothing they could do to help him cope. Bret met Jesus in that journey in such a powerful way that he found focus and peace only in abiding in Jesus. The rest he found in abiding allowed him to study, learn, and function socially.

Bret was a broken man, hungry for Jesus. He was intent on knowing all there was to know about God. When he and I (Jimmy) talked for the first time, the presence of the Lord filled the car. Throughout Bret's college years, we met regularly to jog together, to talk about God and the Spirit, and to worship and pray together in the mornings. More and more, Bret entered into the power and joy that God had for him.

These two humble people, Jackie and Bret, met and soon discovered that they had kindred hearts and minds about living wholeheartedly for Jesus. Eventually, they married, having a common heart for the nations and being willing to do whatever God had for them. On their honeymoon, they took one day to visit the Epcot Center (now Epcot theme park) at Disney World. They wanted to visit the Asia section because they knew God had called them to Asia. As they watched a film about a nation in the Himalayas and about Mongolia, the presence of the Lord surrounded them. With tears flowing, they stayed in the movie theater for three showings, as other people filed in and out.

Jackie and Bret were part of an original team that had led college Lifegroups back in 1990. In those groups, the students learned how to disciple, evangelize and reproduce the life of Christ. Jackie and Bret multiplied their group four different times and were diligent to serve wherever possible in our growing movement.

One day, as Bret walked out of work, a lady who had been praying for him approached him and asked about Mongolia. When she did, the presence of the Lord touched him in such a strong way he had to lean against the wall for support in order not to fall over. He went home and shared the experience with Jackie, and the presence of the Lord touched her as well. They realized that it was time to go.

After finishing the missions training school in 1993, Bret and Jackie led a team sent to Ulaanbaatar, Mongolia, to see a church established. During the early days, they saw a good number of college students come to Christ, and they began to meet from house to house. Though they saw fruit, they found it difficult to develop leaders and see people persevere in their newly found faith.

Bret and Jackie began to pray and ask God for a man of peace—someone who would rise up to take leadership among the people to move them forward. Around that time, Jackie developed a relationship with a neighbor, Chuka. Chuka was a broken and desperate lady, having lived with the difficulties of having an alcoholic husband. Through her relationship with Jackie, she heard the gospel and came to Christ. Jackie began teaching Chuka to pray for her husband, Tsolgi. Bret began to engage Tsolgi in conversations about God's wisdom for the family, as found in Scripture, and about Jesus. After many times of worship together, prayer for Tsolgi, and one key time of spiritual warfare, Jackie, Bret and Chuka eventually saw Tsolgi give his heart to Jesus.

As Bret discipled Tsolgi, he told him that he needed to share Christ with his family. The first person Tsolgi shared with was his mother. This 70-year-old woman was a devout Marxist, teaching Marxism at the only medical school in the nation. Every medical student in Mongolia had to take her class. When she heard the message of Jesus and saw the changed lives of Tsolgi and Chuka, she also gave her life to Christ. As passionate as she had been about Marxism, she became about Jesus. She led 17 adult members of her family to the Lord. This family became the core of multiple cell groups all over the city. God did signs and wonders in their midst, and many were saved.

While God was doing great things among them, this new church knew there was more. They began to pray for the villages and towns that had never heard the gospel. Then they took a short-term trip to another city in Mongolia. After the mission team shared with 200 people, 50 gave their hearts to the Lord and began meeting from house to house.

Over the ensuing years, Bret and Jackie handed the work over to a team of national leaders. Today, the church has spread to 15 different locations with multiple house churches in those locations. A church-planting movement is spreading in Mongolia.

Dead Man Walking

In 2006, we received testimony about a village of 12,000 that the Mongolian church was trying to reach. The Mongolian believers were going into the town regularly to evangelize and reach out to the neighbors and friends of residents who had become Christians. During their visits, they had heard of a man who was very sick and dying of liver cancer.

On one visit to the village, they found that this man (not a Christian yet) had died. For 38 hours, he had no signs of life, so the doctors said to take him home for burial. All the man's family had gathered and were preparing for the funeral.

One of the Mongolian believers thought God wanted her to go and pray for the dead man. However, the family was Buddhist and did not allow it. They actually thought at first that she was making fun of them. But, the man's mother finally relented and allowed the believer to pray for her dead son.

The Mongolian believer placed her hand on the dead man and prayed for him to live. His eyelids moved some, but nothing else happened. Then, she and the other believers left the village and went back to the capital city.

The following week, this believer and a few others returned to the small village, and the "dead" man was there waiting for them . . . ALIVE. He said that he had been dead—"there was nothing at all"—but when she prayed for him, he suddenly heard her praying in Jesus' name and saw a brilliant, bright light. Then, his consciousness returned, but he could not move. He tried to speak to her as she prayed, but he couldn't move at all. After she left the house, his strength slowly returned.

He asked for something to drink about four hours after the prayer, and his family was shocked because a *dead man* was talking to them.

Then he got out of bed and started walking around the town looking for "the Jesus people." His family was astonished that the man they thought was dead was up and speaking, asking them where "the Jesus people" were.

When the newly living man found "the Jesus people," he prayed to receive Jesus and was baptized. His family, all of whom where Buddhist and previously had no interest in Jesus, also prayed and were baptized. A total of 14 people were baptized together with him, including his wife, the doctor who had pronounced him dead, family members, and other villagers!

This man is a 47-year-old taxi driver, well known by the people in the village. It appears that all 12,000 people in the village have now heard about the miracle God worked in his life.

A freshman with an eating disorder and a young man with a physical disability said, "Jesus is enough. He is my portion and my cup. I will not let go of the hem of His garment. I will find my inheritance in Christ alone and give myself to the nations of the earth." They went from wounded freshmen at college to seeing a church-planting movement established and the dead raised. Today, Bret, Jackie and their children live in the Himalayas, ministering to two other unreached people groups and believing for another church-planting movement to be established.

They Followed God's Call to the Nations

Tobias Oloo was a vibrant member of the DOVE Nairobi church in the early '90s, but was also restless due to a call from the Lord on his life to plant churches. After Tobias had served and been nurtured in DOVE Nairobi for some time, the elders recognized this call and commissioned him to plant a DOVE church in the Kibera slum. Meetings started in a small rented room, and the ministry grew steadily. People found not only spiritual nurture, but also genuine love being expressed in practical ways such as food distribution, home visits, and children's ministry. This group of believers also started a school for children called Desert Streams.

In their commitment to the Great Commission, Tobias and his wife, Judy, have also initiated a church plant and community project in Migori, a town in Western Kenya. In addition, they managed to cross the border into Tanzania to spread the gospel of Jesus and disciple new believers there. Previously, Tanzania was the only country in East Africa that DOVE had not reached. All of this has happened one person at a time.

God has used this couple to reach out to a frustrated and dying world through evangelism, care and social action. They have walked in unity to advance God's Kingdom in Kibera, Migori, and now in Tanzania, using whatever resources God has entrusted to their care. The world around them can see God's love practically demonstrated through them.

Phillip Omondi left his homeland of Kenya for India 15 years ago in search of a university education. What he found there, in addition to a degree in law, was a life calling to serve God in India.

While at university, Phillip was active in student fellowships and Bible studies. He soon emerged as a leader. By the time he graduated, he realized that his passion for ministry was stronger than his desire to work as a lawyer. He looked for ways to "buy time" in India, for instance by continuing with a few extra courses that would make it possible for him to extend his student visa. A similar thing happened with a Kenyan young lady in the student fellowship, Kerina, who was also studying law. Phillip and Kerina found themselves in ministry together, leading people to Jesus and discipling them, and later the two married. The student fellowship moved from an on-campus to an off-campus ministry, and then became a church.

Today, Phillip and Kerina pastor Destiny Center in Mysore, India. Many students from local universities, especially African students, are now involved in the church. But local Muslim-background and Hindu-background families are also being reached, and actually are the main "target" for prayer and witness. Mr. Singh and his family are one such target family. The Singhs converted from Hinduism to Christianity in the 1990s. But trials and opposition drove them back to Hinduism. Soon after, Mr. Singh's father became paralyzed and mentally unstable. Then his sister was not able to conceive, his aunt fell sick, and the family businesses were closing one after the other. The family was devastated.

Nearly 10 years later, Mr. Singh started attending Destiny Center with some friends. Phillip and Kerina began praying for him and his family and visiting their home. Through the love and concern of these believers, the family came back to Christ. Soon after that, the first miracle occurred: Mr. Singh's sister became pregnant.

The Hindu gods do not perform miracles. The Hindu gods do not love those who worship them. But Jesus does! As Mr. Singh's family, the believers at Destiny Center, and other families who have come out of Hinduism join in prayer, there is faith for many more miracles to take place in Mysore. Lives are being transformed, one at a time.

Transformation!

Our God is a King who is building His Kingdom in our lives and in our communities. He transforms whole societies as people come to know Him by receiving His good news. I (Larry) recently witnessed God's Kingdom influence in amazing ways during a visit to a new church near Kisumu, Kenya, the birthplace of President Obama's father. At Restoration Church, in the village of Kadawa, I saw firsthand a village of 10,000 being transformed by the kingdom of God! Restoration Church is less than two years old and already has more than 500 people coming together each Sunday. Those who have received Christ also meet during the week in homes throughout the community for prayer and to learn how to experience practical Christianity. In fact, this recently established church has already planted two additional churches with more small groups.

But the most amazing thing is the way the entire community is being transformed by the kingdom of God. Believers are starting new businesses, the swamp in the region has become a banana plantation, and the main government leader of the village and his whole family have been transformed by Christ. This leader told me that his job is now easy because violence and muggings have stopped. Hope has been restored. This is the first year that they can remember when no one has contracted cholera in their community. Last year the community was dying of AIDS, and, while AIDS is still a problem, this year there are signs of Kingdom influence everywhere!

Jim and Patty are team leaders with DOVE's outreach to an unreached people group in Northern Kenya.[1] Both Jim and Patty grew up in the Nairobi area. God has given them a divine call to reach the Muslim world by living in a way that reflects God's Kingdom and His glory. Through simple one-on-one sharing and practical service, closed doors have opened and the gospel of Jesus is penetrating this people group.

Jim and Patty have developed tremendous favor among the tribe. Leaders of this group admit that Islam has blinded and oppressed them to the extent that they could not make their own decisions. In terms of development, they have been behind for several generations. Many people in Kenya do not even know that this particular tribe even exists. Jim and Patty are the ones who have caused this community to be recognized. They have been able to advocate for them and negotiate for projects in the community such as schools, adult education, agriculture and even a medical clinic. The community has learned to trust this couple. The relationships they've built have opened the doors for this people group, which violently resisted previous mission attempts, to be reached.

Patty started a school for the young children in the village in the year 2000. It began under a tree. Her vision was to fight illiteracy in the community and in this way show them the love of Christ. Today, the DOVE preschool is among the best preschools around. Children receive good education and tender care, and they also hear about Jesus and learn Christian moral values. Patty also introduced adult education to help combat the high illiteracy rate.

Several years into their stay in this community, Jim was elected to be an elder in the tribe. This is a position of great honor. It is unheard of for an outsider to be given such a position of leadership. Through working closely with the tribal leaders, Jim and Patty have had so much influence on the chief's life that he now openly displays a Bible on his desk and welcomes Christian groups to come and work among his tribesmen.

A new medical clinic in the village is yet another intervention that Jim and Patty have spearheaded. When the clinic is complete and operating, it will be a tremendous relief to the community, as it is the only medical facility that is practically accessible.

Jim and Patty have found favor with God and men. They have been advocates for this group of people who were previously unreached and have been inspiring role models for other missionaries. Six African DOVE missionaries are now serving with them. And it all started under a tree with a young girl who loved Jesus, loved God's people, and loved the unreached.

God still leads people to the throne of grace—helping, healing and restoring just as He did in the book of Acts. All over the world, believers who love and trust Jesus with abandon are experiencing the supernatural power of God in astounding ways. God's power is not a thing of the past; it is available to us today. And the same God who is doing amazing things among His people in Asia, Africa, and the uttermost parts of the earth desires to do these same things in America. It is up to us. If we respond to Him in faith, our families and towns and cities and communities will also be transformed by the power of Christ through us as we love Him, love His people, and love the lost.

Note
1. Names have been changed for security reasons.

10

Fan the Flame!

Why now is the time to return to the joy of simple and authentic Christianity

Now is the time for us all to return to experiencing the joy of simple and authentic Christianity. Let's expect the Lord to ignite a new passion in us to focus on His priorities! Our humble prayer is that this book will be a tool that the Lord will use to ignite a passion and a flame for genuine spiritual revival in America.

The true stories in this book are only a few of the thousands of stories of how God birthed His desires for nations and people in the hearts of those in our midst. Some stories we can't tell, because doing so would jeopardize those who are serving in closed countries in the world. But wherever they serve, we know that God's desires are becoming reality: the values of simply loving God, each other, and the lost in the context of community are being reproduced all over the world.

Along with a desire to see the world won to Christ, our focus must be on living from the inside out. That is, the things that we proclaim to the world must be the things that we have seen, heard and touched ourselves. Because we have met Jesus and found the life-giving power of His Kingdom, we want to reproduce His values in the lives of people everywhere so that they too can know Him and make Him known—until the whole world hears and knows. And just like the early disciples, we desire to be known as a people who have been with Jesus.

God has called us to be a people who are passionately pursuing Jesus with all of our hearts and deeply committed to His purposes. God doesn't just want to change what we do but also who we are. The doing will flow out of the being. Our desire is not just to be, and it is not just to do. We want a life of obedience and faith that flows out of a deep place of intimacy with Jesus. Learning to love Him in a world that desperately needs Him is how we can be a part of God's plan to change this world.

Two thousand years ago, Jesus stepped into a world that looked a lot like today's world: oppressive political powers, a religion of rules rather than relationship, the rich refusing to distribute the goodness of God to the poor, and multitudes of people distressed and downcast. Jesus showed up to right all of these wrongs. By coming to earth Himself, God showed the world who He really is and set His redemptive plan in motion.

Jesus shocked people when He proclaimed the message of a new Kingdom because what He was saying was so radical. This Kingdom wasn't about "dos and don'ts" but about love, healing and forgiveness. It was about doing what was right out of a relationship with the One who is right. It had everything to do with a God who wanted to connect with people instead of a God who wanted to distance Himself from His creation.

And with that radical message, Jesus extended a radical invitation: Follow Me. Though some rejected Him, others left everything in order to follow Him. That radical response allowed an unlikely group of folks—fishermen, tax collectors, harlots, people from every walk of life—to become Jesus' most intimate friends. As He interacted with these followers day after day, He taught them about His Kingdom and invested in them so they could one day take His message to the world. Jesus even prophesied that He would build His Church and that the gates of hell would not prevail against it.

Perhaps the hardest thing for His followers to grasp was Jesus' teaching about His own death. He told them that unless He died—unless He shed His blood, unless He gave His life on a cross—they would not be able to enter into all that He had for them. No matter how hard they tried to be good enough for God, it would never be enough. They needed a sacrifice. Jesus was that sacrifice. He hung on that cross even as some of these friends denied Him and ran away. He suffered tremendous pain and shame, and with His final breath, He asked God to forgive those who killed Him.

It didn't end there though. Three days later, Jesus rose from the dead. And when He did, it proved once and for all that death would never have power over anyone who would believe. Jesus went back to His friends, the very ones who had failed Him just a few days earlier, and restored them. He reminded them about His Kingdom. And, finally, it made sense to them. Before it had been cool to hang out with Jesus, but they never fully understood what He was talking about until He rose from the dead.

The reality of the Kingdom—of everything Jesus had ever said to them—so transformed them that they were willing to give their own lives for Jesus' message. Jesus' friends and followers became His value carriers, carrying the values He had imparted to them and reproducing them in the next generation.

Just before Jesus ascended into heaven, He told His followers, "But you will receive power when the Holy Spirit comes upon you. And you will be my witnesses, telling people about me everywhere—in Jerusalem, throughout Judea, in Samaria, and to the ends of the earth" (Acts 1:8). With faith, 120 of them gathered to pray and wait for Jesus' promise to be fulfilled.

On Pentecost, the power of God came so heavily that it shook the place they were in. Each one of the 120 was filled with the Holy Spirit and went out to the streets prophesying and speaking in the different languages of the people in the city. These early believers told of the glory of God and the goodness of His heart toward all people. Peter jumped up and preached a phenomenal message. Those listening were amazed, and their hearts were cut to the quick. "What must we do?" they cried out. Peter told them to repent and be baptized—and 3,000 of them did (see Acts 2:1-41).

In one day, the Church was born. Jesus had spoken of this: the ingathering of the people of God and the ongoing reality of those people living together in communion with Him and with one another so that His life could be reproduced all over the world. Those disciples who had walked with Jesus remembered that He had said, "Now I say to you that you are Peter (which means 'rock'), and upon this rock I will build my church, and all the powers of hell will not conquer it" (Matt. 16:18). They were seeing the first fruits of Jesus' prophecy.

Jesus loves His Church . . . He died for it. And as we see through the rest of the book of Acts, the Church loved Him, too. They were on fire for Him. Having heard His radical message, they responded radically and became His Church. Both Larry and I love to read in the pages of the New Testament about who the Church is and what it looks like. Beginning on Pentecost, by the gospel of Jesus Christ and the power of the Holy Spirit, God gathered to Himself a people who were, and today continue to be, the fullness of Christ (see Eph. 1:23), the Body of Christ (see Acts 9:4-6; 1 Cor. 12:27), a spiritual house made up of living stones (see 1 Pet. 2:4-5), the family of God (see Eph. 3:14-19), the bride of Christ (see Eph. 5:25-31), the administration of the gospel (see Eph. 3:8-9), the army of God (see Joel 2:11), the pillar and support of the truth (see 1 Tim. 3:15), the eternal purpose of God in Christ (see Eph. 3:10-11), and so much more.

What we see in Acts 2 is huge. By empowering His followers with His Spirit, Jesus established His Church so that He could walk in close relationship with them, so that they could live in tight community with one another, and so that He could draw the whole world to Himself. Over the years, we've fallen in love with Jesus and His Church; you can't have one without the other. You can't say that you love Jesus but not His people and purposes—they are not separate.

Once those first 120 were multiplied to 3,000, Peter and the apostles immediately gathered them from house to house so that they could learn how to follow Jesus as the Church. Acts 2:42-47 describes what the early days of the Church looked like:

> All the believers devoted themselves to the apostles' teaching, and to fellowship, and to sharing in meals (including the Lord's Supper), and to prayer. A deep sense of awe came over them all, and the apostles performed many miraculous signs and wonders. And all the believers met together in one place and shared everything they had. They sold their property and possessions and shared the money with those in need. They worshiped together at the Temple each day, met in homes for the Lord's Supper, and shared their meals with great joy and generosity—all the while praising God and enjoying the goodwill of all the people. And each day the Lord added to their fellowship those who were being saved.

These people who had said "yes" to the message of the Kingdom were beginning to experience the reality of the Kingdom.

What the Church is and should be is this: believers gathering house to house, praying, studying the Word, experiencing a sense of equality and humility, seeing signs and wonders, feeling the awe of God, and adding to their number day by day.

In those early days, as they lived out the values of the Kingdom before the whole city, Jesus' disciples gained a reputation in Jerusalem. Acts 4:13 says, "The members of the council were amazed when they saw the boldness of Peter and John, for they could see that they were ordinary men with no special training in the Scriptures. They also recognized them as men who had been with Jesus." The first Church was known simply as a people who had been with Jesus. Day by day, they experienced Him and walked out His life together, and the world around them took notice.

Peter and the Acts 2 Church were having a great time together in Jerusalem, so much so that they forgot Judea, Samaria, and the uttermost parts of the earth that Jesus had mentioned before He ascended into heaven. So, in His mercy, God allowed a little persecution to come and help them move on with His purposes.

The church at Jerusalem was threatened, Christians were imprisoned, and some were even killed. The believers prayed about how to respond, and by the will and direction of God, some stayed in Jerusalem to see the church grow to 10,000, but others left. These did not flee simply because they were scared but because God led them.

As they went, they preached the same message they had heard in Jerusalem: the message of the Kingdom. And no matter where they traveled, they lived out the same kind of church community they had lived out in Jerusalem: house-to-house fellowship, worship, prayer, experiencing God, and seeing Him move powerfully in their midst. Because they faithfully carried the values of the Kingdom everywhere they went, they saw the

Church spread to Judea and Samaria and all over Asia.

Throughout the book of Acts, we see churches becoming hubs where laborers were released, received back, refueled, and sent out again. This movement was so effective that in Acts 19:10, it says that all of Asia had heard the gospel. And they had heard not just about Jesus, but about Jesus and His Church—people on fire for God, embodying the values of the Kingdom, and corporately expressing those values to rightfully distribute the gospel. This is the way that the world will be won today: by the Church being the Church, carrying and imparting Kingdom values.

For the original disciples, the simple values of knowing Jesus and making Him known allowed them to endure persecution, to find joy in suffering, to experience power in their ministry, and to see the world changed. John said, "We proclaim to you the one who existed from the beginning, whom we have heard and seen. We saw him with our own eyes and touched him with our own hands. He is the Word of life. This one who is life itself was revealed to us, and we have seen him. And now we testify and proclaim to you that he is the one who is eternal life. He was with the Father, and then he was revealed to us. We proclaim to you what we ourselves have actually seen and heard so that you may have fellowship with us. And our fellowship is with the Father and with his Son, Jesus Christ" (1 John 1:1-3). This wasn't a religion of dead works, but a people who had experienced the real God with their hands, eyes and ears.

Everyday Walk with God

In the early days of our (Jimmy's) church, we met for a time at a place called Melody Ranch, a local country and western bar. It was a lot of fun, and we felt right at home walking into the smells that came with meeting in a bar. In weeks past, we had used a six-foot horse trough for baptisms. We just took the trough with us wherever we met, filled it with water, and baptized people in it. The guy at Melody Ranch told me that instead of bringing our own, we could use the horse trough they used for beer. What he failed to tell us was that his was only a four-foot trough and not a six-foot one like ours.

Several people wanted to be baptized that morning at Melody Ranch, including a local anesthesiologist. When he had invited his family to witness him testify of the goodness of the Lord, he did not know that we would be meeting at Melody Ranch. His family had not come from an Antioch-style background; they were more of a formal bunch. There, on the back row, in their Sunday best, they watched as I literally stuffed this grown man into a four-foot trough. For our congregation, this was a hilarious and joy-filled occasion, and I think even the doctor enjoyed it. He was a great sport, testifying of what the Lord had done for him.

Somehow, the local newspaper had heard about our crazy church and sent a reporter to do a story about us. She was at Melody Ranch the morning of the four-foot horse trough baptisms. It just so happened that we were sharing our vision that morning: We want to be everyday, normal people who live out the simple things of the Kingdom with all of our hearts. We explained that if we will just do that, we can change the world.

The reporter's article, "Everyday Walk with God," landed on the front page of the paper. She did a great job capturing our heart. For us, it seemed like a prophetic message to our city that expressed our desire to be a simple community that walks every day with Jesus as we serve a big God. The irony was that the reporter was not a believer at the time. God used her to get our message out to our city even though she didn't agree with us.

Eventually, she joined our church and began loving Jesus with all of her heart.

It's Real People Who Change the World

Susan met Wanda at "Urban Night," an evening event we sponsor four times a year to get to know and bless our neighbors. Here is Susan's testimony of meeting one of these precious people in our community:

> My husband and I were sitting there listening to the band, and after it stopped I thought, "Well, I'm here to get to know some people," so I started talking to the lady sitting behind me. I asked her if she was a member of Antioch, and she said, "No." We kept talking, and she told me how she had been told about Urban Night by some other people in the neighborhood. She said she really had not wanted to come that night, but something had prompted her to come, so she got ready. Once she was ready, she decided she wasn't going to go, but again, there was a prompting to go, even if she didn't feel like it. She had arrived very late into the event. Eventually I asked her if she knew the Lord, to which she replied that she wasn't sure; there were a lot of things she didn't understand and she didn't know for sure. I asked her if she wanted to be sure, and Wanda replied, "Yes." We walked over to the prayer tent, and Sherry explained things further to Wanda, and we both prayed with her to receive Jesus. The very next day we met for church.
>
> We exchanged e-mails, and through e-mail Wanda just poured her heart out to me. We decided that we

would do some discipleship lessons together. Although Wanda didn't know a lot about the Bible, she was so hungry to learn about Jesus. Soon it got to the point that we needed more personal space to meet in, and we began meeting in her house.

In one of the discipleship lessons, we talked about forgiveness. Wanda had been estranged from her daughter for two years, although she was allowed to see her grandchildren. Now she brings all eight grandchildren to Antioch with her. Wanda's daughter began seeing such a change in her mother that they reconciled, and she occasionally comes to church as well. The daughter commented that every other church she had been to usually remarked on the number of kids she had, but she has felt respected and comfortable at Antioch. I had the privilege of praying with Wanda's daughter when she rededicated her life to Jesus one Sunday. Wanda's husband also said he noticed a change in Wanda's life, and he also occasionally attends Antioch.

I feel like this relationship has been as much a blessing to me as it has been to anybody else. It has taught me a lot, and I have learned that God doesn't ask us to do what we are capable of doing; He only asks us to do what He is capable of doing through us.

Believe for the Impossible

God has always called us to believe Him for the impossible—to see Him as bigger than ourselves.

Who has measured the waters in the hollow of His hand,
And marked off the heavens by the span,

And calculated the dust of the earth by the measure,
And weighed the mountains in a balance
And the hills in a pair of scales?
Who has directed the Spirit of the Lord,
Or as His counselor has informed Him?
With whom did He consult and who gave Him under-
    standing?
And who taught Him in the path of justice and taught
    Him knowledge
And informed Him of the way of understanding?
Behold, the nations are like a drop from a bucket,
And are regarded as a speck of dust on the scales;
Behold, He lifts up the islands like fine dust.
Even Lebanon is not enough to burn,
Nor its beasts enough for a burnt offering.
All the nations are as nothing before Him,
They are regarded by Him as less than nothing and
    meaningless (Isa. 40:12-17, *NASB*).

Isn't it awesome to know that God measures the waters in His hands, weighs the mountains in a balance, and sees the nations as a drop in a bucket? This understanding has caused us to believe that God can do the impossible and will always make a way for us, whether through new strategies or divine appointments.

God has called us to be pioneers, to walk by faith and not by sight, and to not worry about what everybody says you can't do, but rather believe that God can make a way for anyone who believes that nations are a drop in a bucket.

The kingdom of God is good news! Religion places rules and regulations on people and brings them into bondage. The kingdom of God transforms individuals, families, towns, cities and nations. God wants to use each of us as His tools to accomplish His purposes. The kingdom of God is within you (see Luke 17:21) and it is like a mustard seed, which is the smallest of seeds. Yet when planted, it grows and becomes the largest of all garden plants, with such big branches that the birds of the air can perch in its shade (see Mark 4:30-32). No matter how small you may feel, His Kingdom is within you! Start where you are, and watch His Kingdom grow through you.

When we read the words of Jesus and the stories of the people of God in the book of Acts, we come to believe that all of us can be a part of this incredible journey and adventure. In our lifetime, we can see the same kind of things happen just by believing and stepping out in faith.

It is encouraging to see how most of the people that God used in the New Testament were initially either fearful and unsure of themselves or prideful and arrogant. When these individuals finally encountered Christ face to face, they were transformed and willing to risk their lives for what they believed in.

These examples helped us and others begin to take the initial steps of faith and overcome our fears. Whether they were steps toward looking for lost tribes in the jungles of New Guinea or steps toward trusting God with our finances, these risks turned out to be the places where we encountered God the most. Hebrews 11:1-2 says, "Faith is the confidence that what we hope for will actually happen; it gives us assurance about things we cannot see. Through their faith, the people in days of old earned a good reputation." We have to reach out beyond what our eyes can see, knowing that our faith is pleasing to God. Even when we miss the mark, if our faith and hearts are bent towards Jesus, we can trust Him to take care of us and restore us because we have pleased Him by stepping out in faith.

God wants passionate lovers of Jesus—people who love His Church in such a way that they can reproduce an Acts 2:42-47 community around the world—to emerge. We are a simple people living out the gospel in our own locations. By being the Church right where we live, we can reproduce the Church anywhere with a few cultural and language adaptations. Because of this, we can then be sent anywhere in the world to reproduce the life of God.

Our prayer is the same for you. We don't want you to get caught up in our stories. We want you to be caught up with a God who loves you passionately. May you find Jesus and His love and never lose your connection to Him. May you be absorbed in Him so that you are encouraged to love Him more as you experience a growing desire to see His purposes fulfilled in and through your life. Look for Jesus and ask Him how you can partner with Him to change the world.

Our prayer for you is that you will receive a vision from the Lord for your life. You are so important to Him. We want you to know that you can love Jesus with all your heart. You can experience Him personally in such a way that others will see Him in your life. You can join with Jesus' Church to proclaim Him to the uttermost parts of the earth. And our prayer for you is that you will love Jesus with a passion, love His people, and love those who need Jesus in their lives. Our God wants to use you to change the world!

God bless you,
Larry Kreider
Jimmy Seibert

Small-Group Leaders' Guide

We encourage you to use this book as a practical tool to lead your Bible study group, home group, small group or Sunday School class into experiencing the three realities of loving Jesus, loving others and loving a broken world. Discuss the following as a group, and/or assign some for homework.

CHAPTER 1
Our Passion for Jesus and His Purposes in the Earth

1. Especially in a new small group, or occasionally in an already established one, encourage everyone to share his or her story of coming to Jesus.

2. Have the group discuss how Larry's and Jimmy's testimonies of coming to Jesus are similar to their own and how are they are different.

3. Ask the group to describe their spiritual search. What were they looking for?

4. Have members briefly describe the first time they realized God was pursuing a relationship with them.

5. Read 1 Corinthians 2:2. Tell the group how this verse has impacted your life.

6. Read Acts 2:42-47. Discuss ways in which your group looks like this biblical community of believers.

CHAPTER 2
A Return to Simplicity

1. Discuss what kind of implications a firsthand relationship with Jesus and His love for us has on our personal lives. How can we intentionally embrace this love for Him and for others?

2. Ask if anyone has a favorite story of a personal encounter with Jesus that they would like to share with the group. Why does this story impact that person?

3. Have the group describe ways that they have been a "value carrier": one who learns from Jesus, makes His values his or her own, and then reproduces those values everywhere he or she goes.

4. To keep Jesus first in our lives, we must take time to listen to God through reading His Word, worship and prayer. Discuss what each of us can do to make sure this happens.

5. Prayer is a key building block of spiritual maturity. Discuss what is one thing each person could do to improve his or her prayer life.

6. Ask if there is a particular method of studying the Scriptures that makes the Bible come alive for those in the group—hear-

ing, reading, studying, memorizing, meditating on Scripture, or something else?

7. Ask the group if they are investing in someone's life by discipling him or her. If not, how might they seek out that kind of relationship?

8. Read Luke 10:27. Discuss why this verse is so important to the process of reproducing Kingdom values wherever we go.

CHAPTER 3
Loving Jesus with a Passion

1. Discuss what areas of your group's walk with Christ have caused them to change to become more like Him. What areas have not changed that need to be surrendered to Him? Ask the members to list any areas they need to surrender.

2. Discuss what single thing the participants can plan to do that will matter the most in 10 years. What will matter the most in eternity?

3. Read John 15:5. Discuss what we need to do to stay attached to the Vine.

4. Have the members describe how their love for Jesus causes them to look outward to those in need in the world.

5. Read 1 John 1:1. Explain how you have met with Jesus and how you are giving Him away.

CHAPTER 4
How Do You Say the Name of Jesus?

1. Ask the members to describe what characterizes their relationship with Jesus? If they talk to Him (in prayer), does He talk back? If so, in what manner?

2. Discuss how each person understands the personal nature of his or her relationship with Jesus.

3. Discuss how each of our relationships with Jesus is unique to our personalities, gifts and experiences.

4. Ask the participants if they have developed a personal prayer life. If so, how do they do it?

5. Read Luke 11:1-4. Discuss how the prayer that Jesus taught His disciples can help each of us grow in our own prayer lives.

CHAPTER 5
Loving God's People

1. Loving people involves guiding them into a deep, practical "walk" with Christ. These people will change the world around them. Jesus taught this in Matthew 28:19-20, and Paul modeled it with Timothy. Read 2 Timothy 2:2 and explain how lives can be changed and multiplied through discipleship.

2. Establishing a meaningful connection and establishing trust are the foundation for building effective discipleship relationships. Discuss how each person has taken the time to invest in another person's life.

3. We should expect the typical Christian, if correctly discipled, to become a "spiritual reproducer" who can train others. Give some tips for helping someone reproduce himself or herself.

4. Discuss how relationships are "fruitful but fragile"? How does this impact discipling another person?

5. Think of some ways that the small group can help those within it to develop a significant personal ministry of evangelism and disciple-making in order to reach the world for Christ.

CHAPTER 6
Pouring Your Life into People

1. Following the model of Jesus to initiate, build and release, we first of all need to prayerfully seek God's wisdom for discernment as to which Christian(s) will benefit from our investment of time and energy. Ask if anyone in the group has initiated a discipleship relationship with anyone else. If not, how will they do it?

2. Discuss how to get to know a person once we are in relationship with him or her. How do we actively listen? Explain how you share thoughts and feelings authentically, with vulnerability, so your disciple feels at ease with you.

3. Discuss what areas of life we should be hoping that the disciple will grow in. Share how you have grown in areas of your life to encourage your disciple. What has God taught you? How has He taught you?

4. Talk about the non-negotiables of a spiritual parenting relationship—prayer, hearing from God, accountability, servanthood and vulnerability—and if they are happening in their discipleship relationship.

CHAPTER 7
Loving Those Separated from God

1. Jesus was comfortable around non-believers. So many times we get caught up in our Christian circles and we lose contact with the world. Discuss how each of us can connect with those in our world who need to hear from Jesus.

2. No one likes to be preached at. However, when we take the time to build a friendship and trust, it becomes easier to share the love of Christ with others. Tell of a time you developed a friendship with someone and led them to the Lord.

3. Evangelism must be intentional. Share various ways you can reach out and tell people that Jesus loves them.

4. Discuss some of the ways in which the group members' church is being a church with a mission at home and abroad.

CHAPTER 8
Reaching Out in Everyday Life

1. Ask the group members to think about what obstacles are keeping them from being more effective in evangelism. How

can those obstacles be left behind as they reach for all God has for them in the days ahead?

2. Ask the members who is the person(s) they most want to see come to Christ. What obstacles are keeping that person from Christ? Take time to bring that person to God in prayer. Ask for the obstacles to be removed. Invite the Holy Spirit to reveal to that person his or her need and the love and power of Jesus.

3. Have the group commit to initiate a time with their *oikos* person in the next few weeks to build the relationship. Some ideas include going to lunch, working out, bowling, golfing, cooking, camping and playing basketball.

4. Break into groups of four to five and pray for the lost in your neighborhood, school, workplace and family.

CHAPTER 9
The Church Changes the World

1. Read Acts 2:42-47. Explain how your church does and doesn't look like this church.

2. Have the group consider whether their fellowship lives out the values of the Kingdom before their city? In what ways is the church a hub where people are being released, received back, refueled and sent out again?

3. Jesus doesn't just want to change what we do but also who we are. Talk about how you are learning to live a life of

obedience and faith that flows out of a deep place of intimacy with Jesus.

4. Discuss how you can recognize and develop your spiritual gifts and experience the supernatural power of God that is available to you today.

CHAPTER 10
Fan the Flame!

1. To live out the basic values of the Kingdom, we have to love God, be men and women of prayer, disciple others, reach out in evangelism and live intentionally in the context of community. Ask the group members to explain how they are doing these things. What could they do to grow in one or more of these areas?

2. Conclude by asking the participants to consider how, 10 years from now, they would like the reading of this book to have influenced their lives. What could they do in the coming days to increase the likelihood of that outcome occurring?

Daily Prayer Guide

The following prayer guide is designed to be used every day as you meet with the Lord in prayer. Use it to share your heart and move toward an increasingly intimate friendship with Jesus. It's designed with prayers and Scriptures to pray as you progress through each part of the Lord's Prayer. Let's begin.[1]

12 Rooms in
Your Personal House of Prayer

Provision Room Give us today our daily bread	**Forgiveness Room** Forgive us our debts	**Freedom Room** As we also have forgiven our debtors	**Protection Room** And lead us not into temptation
Surrender Room Your will be done, on earth as it is in heaven	"I will . . . give them joy in my house of prayer . . . for my house will be called a house of prayer for all nations." Isaiah 56:7		**Warfare Room** But deliver us from the evil one
Declaration Room Your kingdom come			**Kingdom Room** For yours is the kingdom
Adoration Room Hallowed be your name	**Family Room** Our Father in heaven	**Exaltation Room** And the glory forever. Amen	**Power Room** And the power

THE FAMILY ROOM
"Our Father in Heaven . . ."

Thank You, Lord, that I can have personal and direct access to You. You are never too busy for me. "Call upon Me and come and pray to Me, and I will listen to you" (Jer. 29:12, NASB).

I'm grateful that I can meet You in the family room and know Your love—You are my Father. Thank You, Lord. I know that You totally love and accept me today because I am Your child. "How great is the love the Father has lavished on us, that we should be called children of God!" (1 John 3:1, NIV).

I know that I am loved by You as my heavenly Daddy, because the Bible tells me so. Lord, I believe in You. "For God so loved the world that he gave his one and only Son, that whoever believes in him shall not perish but have eternal life" (John 3:16, NIV).

You know my needs, cares, temptations and problems today. I come boldly to You in my time of need. "Let us then approach the throne of grace with confidence, so that we may receive mercy and find grace to help us in our time of need" (Heb. 4:16).

Lord, Your Word is filled with power. "For the word of God is living and active. Sharper than any double-edged sword, it penetrates even to dividing soul and spirit, joints and marrow; it judges the thoughts and attitudes of the heart" (Heb. 4:12, NIV).

Thank You for transforming me by Your love, so I can freely serve others. "As the Father has loved Me, I have also loved you" (John 15:9, NASB); "Serve one another in love" (Gal. 5:13).

Pray with an open Bible. Fill your prayers with God's Word. Meditate on it. Add additional Scriptures to meditate on and prayers to pray.

Take a few minutes to be still before the Lord. He is your Father; you are His child. Observe if He gives you any more impressions of His love for you. Write them down in your journal along with any prayer requests, Scriptures or answers to prayer.

THE ADORATION ROOM
"Hallowed Be Your Name . . ."

Lord, Your name is holy. Here in the adoration room, I bless Your holy name. "Who among the gods is like you, O Lord? Who is like you—majestic in holiness . . . ?" (Exod. 15:11, NIV); "Holy, holy, holy, is the Lord of hosts" (Isa. 6:3, NASB); "Bless his holy name" (Ps. 103:1, NASB).

Jesus, I exalt Your name above all other names—the most powerful name in heaven and earth. "Therefore God exalted him to the highest place and gave him the name that is above every name, that at the name of Jesus every knee should bow . . . and every tongue confess that Jesus Christ is Lord, to the glory of God the Father" (Phil. 2:9-11, NIV).

Speak the names of God that answer your specific need right now. For example: Jesus, You are my provider (Gen. 22:14); peace (Judg. 6:24); righteousness (Jer. 23:6; 33:16); healer (Exod. 15:26; Jer. 3:22; 30:17; Isa. 61:1, NIV); sanctifier (Exod. 31:13, NASB; Lev. 20:7-8, NASB); shepherd (Ps. 23); and banner (Exod. 17:15). Lord, thank You that You are Wonderful Counselor, Mighty God, Everlasting Father, and Prince of Peace (Isa. 9:6).

You are in a class by Yourself, Lord—awesome and great, the Creator of the entire universe, completely other than what I am. " 'For My thoughts are not your thoughts, nor are your ways My ways,' declares the Lord. 'For as the heavens are higher than the earth, so are My ways higher than your ways and My thoughts than your thoughts' " (Isa. 55:8-9, NASB).

Lord, today's encounter with You changes me, those I pray for, and those I meet today in an ever-increasing way. "And we, who with unveiled faces all reflect the Lord's glory, are being transformed into his likeness with ever-increasing glory, which comes from the Lord, who is the Spirit" (2 Cor. 3:18, NIV).

Take a few minutes to be still before the Lord. Observe if He gives you any more impressions of who He is in your life. Write them down in your journal along with any prayer requests, Scriptures or answers to prayer. Tell God you love Him and adore Him in the adoration room. Reflect on His greatness (see Ps. 8:1-9).

THE DECLARATION ROOM
"Your Kingdom Come . . ."

Here in the declaration room, I thank You for the new Kingdom You set up in my heart when I was born again. "I tell you the truth, no one can see the kingdom of God unless he is born again" (John 3:3, NIV).

I declare that Your Kingdom comes as I submit my life to You. Change me from the inside out as I seek first Your Kingdom. "But seek first his kingdom and his righteousness, and all these things will be given to you as well" (Matt. 6:33, NIV).

I stand in the victory that You have won for me and choose to walk in righteousness, peace and joy. "For the kingdom of God is not a matter of eating and drinking, but of righteousness, peace and joy in the Holy Spirit" (Rom. 14:17, NIV).

I declare Your Word over myself, my family, my church, my community, my nation, my circumstances, and my finances. Lord, help me to see how we all need to change to be more what You want. "For the word of God is living and active" (Heb. 4:12, NIV); "The prayer of a righteous man is powerful and effective" (Jas. 5:16, NIV).

I pray for my church and for my spiritual leaders that they would be filled with wisdom and spiritual understanding. "I keep asking that the God of our Lord Jesus Christ, the glorious Father, may give you the Spirit of wisdom and revelation, so that you may know him better" (Eph. 1:17, NIV).

I pray for the president and other government officials that they would seek God for wisdom so they are effective in office. "I urge, then, first of all, that requests, prayers, intercession and thanksgiving be made for everyone—for kings and all those in authority, that we may live peaceful and quiet lives in all godliness and holiness" (1 Tim. 2:1-2, NIV). "The king's heart is like channels of water in the hand of the LORD; He turns it wherever He wishes" (Prov. 21:1, NASB).

I pray for missionaries to clearly communicate the gospel to those they want to reach. (Pray for their personal needs: health, safety, and victory over discouragement and loneliness.)

Now declare "who you are in Christ":

> I am now God's child (see 1 John 3:2).
> I am born of the imperishable seed of God's Word (see 1 Pet. 1:23).

I am loved by Christ and freed from my sins (see Rev. 1:5).
I am forgiven all my sins (see Eph. 1:7).

Take a few minutes to be still before the Lord. He is your God; you are His co-laborer. Observe if He gives you any more impressions of areas He may be calling you to declare. Write them down in your journal along with any prayer requests, Scriptures or answers to prayer.

THE SURRENDER ROOM
"Your Will Be Done, on Earth as It Is in Heaven."

Lord, in the surrender room, I invite You into my life here on earth and give up everything that keeps me from wanting Your ways first. "Father... not my will, but yours be done" (Luke 22:42, NIV).

I seek first Your Kingdom (see Matt. 6:33) so that Your Kingdom comes to all people. I pray that everyone You have placed in my life receives the benefit of living on a planet where Your will is done! This includes [list people, benefits or things that God wills to be done on earth].

I surrender all to You and acknowledge You as Lord over all areas of my life. "Lean not on your own understanding; in all your ways acknowledge him, and he will make your paths straight" (Prov. 3:5-6, NIV).

Surrendering may involve waiting. Lord, I will wait in silence, alert to what You may say to me. "My soul waits in silence for God" (Ps. 62:1, NASB); "My soul waits for the Lord more than watchmen wait for the morning" (Ps. 130:6, NIV); "Those who wait on the Lord shall renew their strength" (Isa. 40:31, NKJV).

Lord, I know that submission and resting go hand in hand. I give You my cares today. I cast them all on You. "Cast all your anxiety on him because he cares for you" (1 Pet. 5:7, NIV).

Lord, may I only take on burdens that You give to me, not those I give myself or those that others give to me. Your yoke is easy and Your burden is light. I give You my cares today. "Come to me, all you who are weary and burdened, and I will give you rest. Take my yoke upon you and learn from me, for I am gentle and humble in heart, and you will find rest for your souls. For my yoke is easy and my burden is light" (Matt. 11:28-30, NIV).

Lord, I choose to be content today no matter what I am going through, as I surrender to You. "For I have learned to be content whatever the circumstances" (Phil. 4:11, NIV).

Take a few minutes to be still before the Lord. He is the King of the universe, and we are His servants. Observe if He gives you any more impressions of areas He may be calling you to surrender to Him. Write them down in your journal along with any prayer requests, Scriptures or answers to prayer.

THE PROVISION ROOM
"Give Us Today Our Daily Bread . . ."

Lord, here in the provision room, I am going to ask for daily bread—for abundant provision. You tell us to ask and that we do not have because we do not ask. "You do not have because you do not ask" (Jas. 4:2, NKJV).

I ask in faith in Jesus' name! "Ask and it will be given to you; seek and you will find; knock and the door will be opened to you. For everyone who asks receives; he who seeks finds; and to him who knocks, the door will be opened" (Luke 11:9-10, NIV).

I depend on You to provide my daily needs like the birds and the wildflowers depend on You (see Matt. 6:25-34).

Lord, You are El Shaddai, the God who is "more than enough." Thank You for doing immeasurably more than all I could even ask or imagine today (see Eph. 3:20).

Your supply is limitless, and abundant blessing is Your nature. "I will look on you with favor and make you fruitful and increase your numbers, and I will keep my covenant with you. You will still be eating last year's harvest when you will have to move it out to make room for the new" (Lev. 26:9-10, NIV).

Thank You for giving me a surplus so that I have extra to give to others (see 2 Cor. 8:14-15; 9:8-11).

Help me to manage my resources, Lord, in a godly way (see Matt. 25:14-30).

Read Psalm 103, and note its list of benefits. Pray these benefits and provisions over your life. Read the promises in Deuteronomy 28.

I claim these promises for my life and for the lives of my loved ones in Jesus' name. I pray for _____

_____, *who is in great need of provision right now. Lord, use me as Your vessel of blessing.*

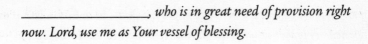

Take a few minutes to be still before the Lord. He is your Father and provider; you are His child. Observe if He gives you any more impressions of areas in which He may be calling you to ask Him for provision, both for you and for others. Write them down in your journal along with any prayer requests, Scriptures or answers to prayer.

THE FORGIVENESS ROOM
"Forgive Us Our Debts . . ."

Lord, here in the forgiveness room, I want You to address three issues in my life—my sin, Your forgiveness of my sin, and how to access that forgiveness through confession.

My sin: *I know that if I harbor sin in my life, I will have trouble communicating with You. Lord, I am in agreement with You regarding any sin in my life (see Ps. 32:3-5). I do not excuse my sin, because I know that sin means I have missed the bull's eye. Anything off the center of Your will is sin.*

Your forgiveness of my sin: *I know You will completely forgive me of my sins (my debts). Your blood cleanses me and makes me pure before You. "But if we walk in the light, as he is in the light, we have fellowship with one another, and the blood of Jesus, his Son, purifies us from all sin" (1 John 1:7, NIV).*

Accessing Your forgiveness by confession: *I ask for Your forgiveness right now. "Forgive my debts!" I confess my sin (admit my guilt). "If I had cherished sin in my heart, the Lord would not have listened; but God has surely listened and heard my voice in prayer. Praise be to God, who has not rejected my prayer or withheld his love from me!* (Ps. 66:18-20, NIV).

I refuse to struggle with false guilt or condemnation. "If we confess our sins, he is faithful and just and will forgive us our sins and purify us from all unrighteousness" (1 John 1:9, NIV).

Here in the forgiveness room, I know that confessing is a daily activity because I am not perfect. "If we claim to be without sin, we deceive ourselves" (1 John 1:8, NIV); "But if anybody does sin, we have one who speaks to the Father in our defense—Jesus Christ, the Righteous One" (1 John 2:1, NIV).

Take time in the forgiveness room to be still before the Lord and ask Him to reveal anything you may have missed. *"See if there is any wicked way in me, and lead me in the way everlasting"* (Ps. 139:24, NKJV).

In your prayer journal, list the areas you know your loving heavenly Father has forgiven you of because of His shed blood on the cross. Also, write down any prayer requests or Scriptures He may be giving to you.

THE FREEDOM ROOM
"As We Also Have Forgiven Our Debtors . . ."

Lord, I realize that a key to finding freedom is forgiving others. "For if you forgive men when they sin against you, your heavenly Father will also forgive you. But if you do not forgive men their sins, your Father will not forgive your sins" (Matt. 6:14-15, NIV).

Search my heart, Lord, to see if there is any unforgiveness there. I don't want a root of bitterness to grow. "See to it that no one misses the grace of God and that no bitter root grows up to cause trouble and defile many" (Heb. 12:15, NIV).

Lord, I forgive _____ (place individuals' names here) in Jesus' name. I know that what they did was wrong, but I ask You to forgive them, and I pray that You will bless them.

Lord, help me to become "offense proof" today. Guard my heart so that I will not look to give offense, nor look to find offense. Restore both me and those I forgive into Your fellowship, Lord.

Help me, Lord, to forgive and receive freedom from You when I am hurt by others. Help me to rejoice in opportunities to show mercy rather than expecting strict justice. "Judgment without mercy will be shown to anyone who has not been merciful. Mercy triumphs over judgment!" (Jas. 2:13, NIV).

Lord, I trust You to set me free as I have forgiven. "Christ redeemed us from the curse of the law by becoming a curse for us" (Gal. 3:13, NIV); "The reason the Son of God appeared was to destroy the devil's work" (1 John 3:8, NIV).

Lord, in Jesus' name I receive Your healing of the memories of what has happened. I am willing to receive prayer from a trusted friend if needed. "Therefore confess your sins to each other and pray for each other so that you may be healed. The prayer of a righteous man is powerful and effective" (Jas. 5:16, NIV).

Lord, I will be patient, knowing the process may not happen overnight. My trust is in You to obtain a full recovery. "Imitate those who through faith and patience inherit what has been promised" (Heb. 6:12, NIV).

In your journal, list areas in which you need freedom. Take a few minutes to be still before the Lord. He is your heavenly Father who has forgiven you completely. You are His beloved child. Observe if He gives you any more impressions of persons He is asking you to forgive. Forgive them, in Jesus' name.

THE PROTECTION ROOM
"And Lead Us Not into Temptation . . ."

Lord, I depend on You to keep me from sin. "Pray that you may not enter into temptation" (Luke 22:40, NASB).

I know You understand temptations I face because You were tempted like me. "For we do not have a High Priest who cannot sympathize with our weaknesses, but was in all points tempted as we are, yet without sin" (Heb. 4:15, NKJV).

I come boldly to You today to find mercy and grace (see Heb. 4:16).

Help me, Lord, not to allow wrong thoughts and actions to gain control and become sin in my life. "But each one is tempted when he is drawn away by his own desires and enticed. Then, when desire has conceived, it gives birth to sin; and sin, when it is full-grown, brings forth death" (Jas. 1:14-15, NKJV).

I know that temptation does not come from You, Lord. "When tempted, no one should say, 'God is tempting me.' For God cannot be tempted by evil, nor does he tempt anyone" (Jas. 1:13, NIV).

Lord, here in the protection room, I ask for Your power to keep me from yielding to temptation. "No temptation has seized you except what is common to man. And God is faithful; he will not let you be tempted beyond what you can bear" (1 Cor. 10:13, NIV).

Protect me today, Lord, from three main areas of temptation: coveting, lust and pride. "For everything in the world—the cravings of sinful man, the lust of his eyes and the boasting of what he has and does—comes not from the Father but from the world" (1 John 2:16, NIV).

Thank You, Lord, for the grace to endure temptation. "Blessed is the man who endures temptation" (Jas. 1:12, NKJV).

Today, I trust You to protect my life and my loved ones from temptation and harm.

Listen to the Holy Spirit as you pray through Psalm 91. Place your name and the names of those you are praying for in the Scripture and claim each promise.

Pray for protection for your family, spiritual leaders, leaders in government, and missionaries. Observe if God gives you any more impressions of individuals He wants you to pray protection over. Write in your journal those times, both present and past, when you know you have experienced the Lord's protection.

THE WARFARE ROOM
"But Deliver Us from the Evil One..."

I bring every thought that I have into captivity to the obedience of Christ today in Jesus' name (see 2 Cor. 10:3-5, NKJV)!

Lord, here in the warfare room, I am aware that I am engaged in a spiritual battle. Satan wants me to fail, but You have guaranteed me victory. Today, I choose to "fight the good fight of faith" (1 Tim. 6:12, NKJV). I put on the whole armor of God today (see Eph. 6:10-17):

> My belt: I have the belt of truth around my waist.
>
> My breastplate: I am righteous through faith in Jesus Christ. I have peace with God through Jesus (see Rom. 5:1).
>
> My shoes: I choose to walk in forgiveness and pursue peace (see Rom. 12:18).
>
> My shield: I take up the shield of faith to protect me from the enemy's fiery darts.
>
> My helmet: I know that I am born again and Jesus has changed my life. My helmet of salvation is secure.
>
> My sword: I take the Word of God boldly and confront the powers of darkness in Jesus' name.

In Jesus' name, I bind up the demonic strongholds in [list the person's name] so that he/she can see the truth (see Matt. 18:18). Lord, I pray that _____'s [name someone you are praying for] eyes are opened so that he/she comes to faith in Christ. Unveil their eyes (see 2 Cor. 4:3-4).

I declare that today "I am more than a conqueror" through Jesus Christ. "We are more than conquerors through him who loved us" (Rom. 8:37, NIV).

Lord, I resist the devil in Jesus' name in this area of my life: [list an area]. He must go (see Jas. 4:7-8)!

Lord, the reason You came was to destroy the work of the enemy. I declare that the works of the enemy over [list an area] are being destroyed in Jesus' name! "The reason the Son of God appeared was to destroy the devil's work" (1 John 3:8, NIV).

In your journal, write down how you have used your spiritual armor recently. Observe if God gives you any more impressions of persons He is calling you to enter into spiritual battle for. Write in your journal those times, both present and past, when you know you have experienced the Lord's deliverance.

THE KINGDOM ROOM
"For Yours Is the Kingdom . . ."

I thank You, my God, that no matter what is going on in my life at this moment, I am a vital part of Your eternal Kingdom that cannot be shaken (see Heb. 12:28-29)!

As I enter the kingdom room, Lord, I commit to You that in everything I say and do today, I will ask, "What would Jesus do?" I thank You that I live as a citizen of Your Kingdom and that I am Your son/daughter (see Eph. 1:3-8).

I am a representative of Your Kingdom on earth, Lord. The Kingdom is within me (see Luke 17:20-21).

Lord, I thank You for Your Kingdom of righteousness, peace and joy in the Holy Spirit in my life today! Is there a lack of Your Kingdom in my life today? "For the kingdom of God is not a matter of eating and drinking, but of righteousness, peace and joy in the Holy Spirit" (Rom. 14:17, NIV).

Lord, give me an outward focus. Here in the kingdom room, I pray for: my family, my business, my community, my church and other churches in my community (for revival), my job, my loved ones, healing for myself and others, the gifts of the Spirit to be developed in my life and in the lives of those around me, the peace of Jerusalem (see Ps. 122), my president or the leader of my nation, my spiritual leaders—pastors, elders and deacons, and unity in the Kingdom (unity among churches).

Pray through Isaiah 43:5-7. It is a powerful prayer to pray over our families, communities, churches and nations.

Ask God to dispatch angels to minister to those from these areas who will inherit salvation (see Heb. 1:13-14). Call them into the Kingdom (see Luke 12:32; Col. 1:12-14). Kingdom praying is not about just our fulfillment but also our transformation and the transformation of those around us.

Write in your prayer journal the names of the people who you are calling into the kingdom of God. Add testimonies, prayer requests and answers to prayer.

Take a few minutes to be still before the Lord. Observe if He gives you any other impressions of areas of your life in which you need to acknowledge His Kingdom that cannot be shaken. Write down in your journal times, both present and past, when you know you have experienced the Lord's stability in the midst of uncertain circumstances.

THE POWER ROOM
"And the Power . . ."

Lord, I need to be plugged into Your power source. I pray for an infilling of Your Spirit in my life today. "For the kingdom of God is not a matter of talk but of power" (1 Cor. 4:20, NIV).

I need Your power. I pray for a new dimension of the Holy Spirit's power in my life and the lives of those I am praying for. "Pray with unceasing prayer and entreaty on every fitting occasion in the Spirit, and be always on the alert to seize opportunities for doing so, with unwearied persistence and entreaty on behalf of all God's people" (Eph. 6:18, Weymouth).

In the power room, take the opportunity to pray, not only in the native language you speak, but also in a spiritual language (your prayer language between God and you), if you have received this gift from the Lord. "I will pray with my spirit, but I will also pray with my mind" (1 Cor. 14:15, NIV).

Lord, I know that praying is not about saying the right words. Holy Spirit, help me to pray earnest prayers (see Rom. 8:26-27). "The prayer of a righteous man is powerful and effective" (Jas. 5:16, NIV). When we pray purposefully, God responds powerfully (see Jas. 5:17-18)!

Lord, all my work for You depends not on human strength but on the power of Your Spirit. "Not by might nor by power, but by my Spirit" (Zech. 4:6, NIV).

Lord, I can't solve my problems or the problems of others by myself. I give You full control. I trust You. My weakness is no obstacle for You (see 2 Cor. 12:9-10)! "Be strong in the Lord and in his mighty power" (Eph. 6:10, NIV).

Lord, I know I need to be filled with Your Spirit again and again. Fill me anew with Your Holy Spirit today.

In Acts 4:31, many of these believers had already been filled with the Holy Spirit at Pentecost (Acts 2). They needed, however, to be filled again. Take a few minutes to be still before the Lord. Observe if He gives you any other impressions of areas of your life or in the lives of others wherein you need to trust in His power to experience victory. Ask the Lord for a fresh infilling of the Holy Spirit today. Add any other Scriptures that you can claim regarding God's power in your life.

THE EXALTATION ROOM
"And the Glory Forever. Amen."

Father, here in the exaltation room, I worship You, and You alone, for who You are: the Lord of all lords and the King of all kings. "Who is this King of glory? The Lord strong and mighty, the Lord mighty in battle" (Ps. 24:8, NIV).

I exalt You and worship You with all my heart. "True worshipers will worship the Father in spirit and truth, for they are the kind of worshipers the Father seeks" (John 4:23, NIV).

Lord, I praise and worship You with my whole spirit, soul and body. "But you are holy, you who inhabit the praises of Israel" (Ps. 22:3, WEB).

Lord, may my life of obedience be a sacrifice of praise and worship to You!

"Through Jesus, therefore, let us continually offer to God a sacrifice of praise—the fruit of lips that confess his name. And do not forget to do good and to share with others, for with such sacrifices God is pleased" (Heb. 13:15-16, NIV).

Lord, expand my vision of You. You are able to do immeasurably more than all I can ask or imagine, according to Your power that is at work within me (see Eph. 3:20). I will express myself in worship to You in the exaltation room through:

> *Kneeling (see Ps. 95:6)*
> *Standing and praising (see Rev. 7:9-10)*
> *Lifting up hands (see 1 Tim. 2:8)*
> *Being still (see Ps. 46:10)*
> *Praising Him with instruments (see Ps. 150:3-5)*
> *Dancing (see Ps. 149:3)*
> *Singing new songs (see Ps. 149:1)*
> *Clapping and shouting (see Ps. 47:1)*

"Speaking . . . in psalms and hymns and spiritual songs, singing and making melody with your heart to the Lord" (Eph. 5:19, *NASB*). Use your favorite worship CD and bask in the Lord's presence.

Singing to the Lord. When you praise the Lord, the enemy is defeated (see 2 Chron. 20:22)!

Listen for the Lord to speak to you about anything else He wants to tell you during your time of prayer. Declare His Lordship over every area of your life. Add answers to prayer, prayer requests and meaningful Scriptures. Observe if He gives you any other impressions of His greatness and His power. Add any other Scriptures that you can use to exalt Him as your Lord and King.

Note

1. See Larry Kreider, *Building Your Personal House of Prayer* (Shippensburg, PA: Destiny Image Publishers, 2008) for more insights on how to pray through the 12 rooms found in the Lord's Prayer.

Recommended Discipleship Training

Use this 12-book *Biblical Foundation Series* as a one-on-one discipling tool. There are multiple ways to use these books:

- *Personal Study:* Read from start to finish as an individual study program to build firm Christian foundations and develop spiritual maturity in your life.
- *Daily Devotional:* Each book gives a month's worth of daily readings with corresponding questions.
- *Mentoring Relationship:* Questions can be answered and life applications discussed as a one-on-one discipling tool.
- *Small-group Study:* Study each book in a small-group setting. Each chapter has a user-friendly teaching outline.
- *Biblical Foundation Course:* Use this series to teach essential biblical foundations at your church.

1. Knowing Jesus Christ as Lord

"I have often wondered, is there a purpose for my being on this earth? Why was I born?"

Understanding God's purpose for our lives through a personal relationship with Jesus Christ is the basic foundation of Christianity (see John 17:3). When we realize we are lost, we must count the cost of commitment, repent of our sins, and confess Jesus as Lord of everything in our lives. To simply say "we believe" is not enough. To believe as God wants us to believe involves total trust. In this first discipleship book, we start with Jesus Christ and His words: "Whoever hears these sayings of Mine, and does them, I will liken him to a wise man who built his house on the rock" (Matt. 7:24, *NKJV*). Do you want to be wise? Build on Jesus Christ, the solid rock! God's purpose for your life is for you to have a personal relationship with Jesus.

2. The New Way of Living

"What are the basic foundations on which we build our lives as Christians?"

In this second book, we look at two of the six foundational doctrines of the Christian faith found in Hebrews 6:1-2—repentance from dead works and faith toward God: "Therefore, leaving the discussion of the elementary principles of Christ, let us go on to perfection, *not laying again the foundation of repentance from dead works and of faith toward God,* of the doctrine of baptisms, of laying on of hands, of resurrection of the dead, and of eternal judgment" (*NKJV*, emphasis added). We will learn that we must repent from trying to gain God's acceptance by doing good things. Good deeds done to impress God or man are "dead works," and they do not get us closer to God. Only true repentance leads to faith in God. True repentance and faith toward God are two spiritual building blocks we need in order to build our lives on a firm foundation. True repentance vs. false repentance is discussed, and faith vs. good works is explained. If we try to please God with good works, He looks on them as filthy rags. The potent mixture of faith and God's Word sets us free.

3. New Testament Baptisms

"I don't understand the different kinds of baptism mentioned in the Bible. What is the purpose for each one?"

In this third book, we look at another of the six foundational doctrines of the Christian faith found in Hebrews 6:1-2—the doctrine of baptisms: "Therefore, leaving the discussion of the elementary principles of Christ, let us go on to perfection, not laying again the foundation of . . . the doctrine of baptisms" (*NKJV*). There are four baptisms mentioned in the Bible: baptism in water, being baptized into the body of Christ, baptism with the Holy Spirit, and baptism with fire. Water baptism (Mark 1:4-5) is a public announcement of our faith in Christ, showing that we are "buried with Christ" (Rom. 6:4), and our old sin nature is cut off (Col. 2:11-12). Being baptized into the Body of Christ (1 Cor. 12:13) occurs when the Holy Spirit supernaturally places us in the wonderful family of God. The baptism with fire (Luke 3:16-17) happens when the Lord allows us to face trials of life that build character in our lives. The baptism in the Holy Spirit (Acts 1:5) is having the power of the Holy Spirit released in our lives.

4. Building for Eternity

"Now that I'm a believer, does how I live my life really matter? Is there a real heaven and hell?"

The three spiritual foundations of "the laying on of hands, the resurrection of the dead, and eternal judgment" (Heb. 6:2, *NIV*) are explained in this book. The laying on of hands covers imparting life to one another, imparting the power of the Holy Spirit, imparting spiritual gifts, imparting health to the sick, and imparting spiritual blessings. We will learn that the laying on of hands has a vital connection to many aspects of our Christian lives. The hope of the resurrection is another biblical foundation that is so important to a Christian's faith because those who believe in Christ will share in His resurrection and have eternal life! Another foundation stone that is linked to the resurrection of the dead is eternal judgment. Every man and woman who has ever lived will be judged by God for all of eternity. The reality of an eternal judgment should cause all believers to hate sin and diligently seek the lost to tell them of God's wonderful plan for humankind!

5. Living in the Grace of God

"What is the grace of God all about?"

In this fifth book, we discover that it is grace that motivates God to offer us salvation even though we did not earn it. In fact, we cannot earn it. Our salvation comes as a gift of God's grace, and it can be accessed by our response of faith. God's grace—the free unmerited favor of God on the undeserving and ill-deserving—is present in our lives to save us. Then we will look at the other side of God's grace, which we define as "the power and desire to do God's will." The grace of God is literally "divine energy" that the Holy Spirit releases in our lives. God has given us supernatural provision to live victorious lives. God gives us an abundance of grace! We do not deserve any of it, but the Lord pours it on us anyway. Christians can do nothing except by the grace of God. It is a free gift, not earned. Grace releases divine energy that empowers us to do His will. When we speak "grace" to a difficult situation in our lives, watch the mountain crumble!

6. Freedom from the Curse

"Somebody once said there was a curse on my life. Is that possible?"

Sometimes Christians have areas of bondage in their lives that they need to address. These are curses in our lives (sickness curse, financial curse, social maladjustment curse, demonic activity curse, mental anguish curse, broken heart curse, etc.). This book explains how a believer can walk in the freedom that Jesus Christ brings because He became a curse for us (see Gal. 3:13). It covers reasons that God allows evil in the world, how Christians must take back from Satan areas of our lives he has stolen, and how to receive and experience wholeness in Jesus' name.

We learn that as a result of Adam and Eve's disobedience to the Lord when they chose to believe the lies of the devil in the Garden of Eden, we now live in a "cursed" or "fallen" world. Through the fall of Adam, sin gained entrance into the human race. In this book, we will take a closer look at all that is involved in the curse and how to be freed spiritually, physically and emotionally from its bondage(s). Although sin has cursed humankind, Christ provides everything we need to defeat sin and Satan!

7. Learning to Fellowship with God

"I was told that God will actually speak to me. How do I hear God's voice?"

This book helps the Christian deepen his or her relationship with God by first understanding who God is (the Trinity is explained) and then learning to build a relationship with Him. By meditating on God's Word, praying, and worshiping Him, we begin to communicate with God. God wants to know us personally! We will discover how to develop a close, intimate relationship with

God through Jesus Christ as we learn to hear His voice. This book stresses communicating with God because we love Him!

8. What Is the Church?

"I love Jesus, but I'm not sure about the Church. How important is it for me to be involved in a local church?"

Because Christians need to encourage one another and be built into a spiritual family, it is important to be linked with other Christians in a local church in addition to the larger Body of Christ. This book covers the concepts of spiritual families and the spiritual protection they offer as a believer relates to the local church. Knowing where God has placed you in the local church and making a commitment to support the local church is discussed and explained from the Scriptures. We will see the importance of being a part of a spiritual family united under Christ. This spiritual family gives us a place to grow and a way to learn from other believers how to live our Christian lives. We need this input from spiritual leaders and fellow believers. We need one another. We are not supposed to live the Christian life alone. God's will is for every believer to be connected to a local church where he or she can be trained, protected, and available to serve others.

9. Authority and Accountability

"Sometimes I find it difficult to submit to authority. Does the Bible say anything about it?"

This book tells how to respond to leadership and other believers God places in our lives (pastors, government authorities, employers, parents, and so forth.). Submission is a heart attitude. How to submit and how to appeal to authority are covered. Accountability helps us see the blind spots in our lives. Personal accountability is finding out from God what He wants us to do and then asking others to remind us to do those things. We learn that the Lord has chosen to give His authority to men and women in various areas, including the government, our employment, the Church, and our families. If we have a healthy understanding of the fear of the Lord, we will understand why God places authorities in our lives. The Lord delegates responsibility to these authorities so that He can use them to bring protection, adjustment and structure into our lives. A proper understanding of authority will bring security into our lives.

10. God's Perspective on Finances

"Does God care about how I handle my money?"

God took a risk when He made us stewards of His money. Our love for it could corrupt us. The importance of giving tithes and offerings is explained. People rob God by not tithing. God will open the windows of heaven and rebuke the devourer when we give to God (see Mal. 3:8-11). Financial blessings allow us to meet more needs around us. Whether we have little or much, we should be content (see Phil. 4:11). In this tenth discipleship book, we learn that God wants to bless us financially! God desires to meet our needs and provide abundantly for us, so that we are able to minister to others. We will learn that the tithe is a numerical expression reminding us that all we have belongs to God. We are merely managers of the material goods we possess. Scripture has a tremendous amount to say about money or material possessions. Money is such an important issue because a person's attitude toward it often is revealing of his or her relationship with God. God wants to restore a healthy, godly understanding of finances in the Body of Christ today.

11. Called to Minister

"I hear people talking about 'God's call on their lives.'
For what purpose has God called me?"

It is every Christian's call to serve. Every saint is called to be a minister (see Eph. 4:11-12; Mark 16:17-18). This book covers the various abilities and ministries God gives us as we partner with Him, as well as the kinds of people God calls to leadership. The Lord has called pastors and other spiritual leaders to train the saints so that every believer can be involved in ministry and become mature in Christ. As each believer fulfills what the Lord has called him or her to do, a wonderful thing happens. God begins to build His Church through His people from house to house and in each community. Ministry does not just happen in our church meetings; it happens in our schools, our places of work, and our homes as we reach out to others.

12. The Great Commission

"If Jesus had any last words for us, I wonder what they would be."

This book covers our purpose for being on this planet. Our marching orders, found in the Great Commission, are to "go."

Wherever we are, we are to go and make disciples. To stay a strong Christian, we must meet daily with the Lord, praying and worshiping Him as we put on our spiritual armor. Then we will be ready to reach the lost. The "*oikos* strategy" of reaching out to friends and relatives causes people to come to Christ and spiritual multiplication to happen. How to make and mentor disciples is also covered in this book. Although some believers will go to another country to make disciples, many believers will reach out to others right where they live. God places all around us people whom we can disciple and train. We will learn what it means to go as a spiritual force (army) to evangelize, make disciples and mentor others, and see the kingdom of God advance! We will discover that an effective way of making disciples is by mentoring others in a spiritual father or mother capacity.[1]

Note

1. This is a synopsis of the 12-book *Biblical Foundation Series* by Larry Kreider, available through House to House Publications, http://www.h2hp.com.

APPENDIX C

How to Share Your Testimony

The apostle Paul set an example for us by taking advantage of many opportunities to share his testimony with others. We can examine one of these occasions—Paul's appearance before King Agrippa—as it is described in Acts 26:4-23. These verses show a clear pattern to use for our own personal testimonies.

Before conversion: In Acts 26:4-11, Paul described his outward sin and his inward need. Having been deeply committed to his Jewish faith, he became obsessed with a passion to defend his religion no matter how wrong his actions might be. His conviction ultimately drove him to persecute the Christian Church and thereby resist the Spirit of God. Being under this conviction of sin (see v. 14), his great need was to admit he had been wrong.

Conversion: In Acts 26:12-18, Paul described how his inward need was met. A description of how Paul met Christ is presented, including an account of where Paul was and what happened to him. God met his need by humbling him and allowing him to see who Jesus really was.

After conversion: In Acts 26:19-23, Paul described how his outward life changed. We read about how Paul obtained Christ's help and began to humbly carry out God's will for his life.

Our personal testimonies can follow this same outline, consisting of:

- Mentioning what the inward need was in our lives, prior to our salvation, that brought us to Christ;
- Describing the circumstance of our conversion and how the inward need was met (i.e., where, when and what happened); and
- Relating how our inward need has now been met after receiving Jesus and how our outward life has changed.

People should hear that we have experienced the same needs they have. These needs are common to all people, though in varying degrees. Christ has met these needs in our lives. In our testimonies, we should be sure to include not only the outward sins that bound us, but also the inward needs that drove us.

Have everyone in your small group write their testimonies and practice sharing them![1]

Note
1. This "How to share your testimony" excerpt was taken from the training manual *Helping You Build Cell Churches,* by Brian Sauder and Larry Kreider (Lititz, PA: House to House Publications, 2000), p. 43.

APPENDIX D

Who God Is

Read one Scripture and worship Him for each aspect of His character.

Father/Creator
Genesis 1–3
Psalm 27:10
Psalm 103:13-18
Psalm 104
Psalm 105
Psalm 139
Isaiah 40:11
Isaiah 49:14-16
Jeremiah 29:11
Jeremiah 31:3,20

Son/Redeemer
Psalm 103:1-6
Isaiah 53
John 1
Colossians 1:14-28

Ephesians 1:19-22
Hebrews 1:1-3
Revelation 1:1-3
Revelation 5

Holy Spirit
Genesis 1:2
Isaiah 61:1-3
Isaiah 11:1-3
Zechariah 4:6
Zechariah 12:10
John 16:7-16
Acts 1:8
Acts 4:31
Romans 8:25-26
1 Corinthians 2:9-16
1 Corinthians 12–14

About the Authors

Larry Kreider loves Jesus and is committed to His purposes in our generation. He currently serves as International Director of DOVE Christian Fellowship International (DCFI), a worldwide network of churches.

At age 18, Larry had an experience with the Lord that led him to begin working with a group of unchurched young people in Lancaster County, Pennsylvania. As the teens made commitments to Christ, they found it difficult to fit in at area churches. To help meet this need, Larry and a team of young leaders planted a new church called DOVE Christian Fellowship in 1980, and Larry served as the senior pastor. Within 10 years, by the grace of God, the church grew from 25 to more than 2,000 members. In 1996, DOVE decentralized from one church into eight different congregations to become an apostolic movement known as DOVE Christian Fellowship International (DCFI). Today DCFI is a growing family of churches and ministries scattered across 18 states and 18 nations in six continents of the world.

During the past two decades, Larry and the team he serves with have trained Christian leaders nationally and internationally to love Jesus passionately, to make disciples and to reach those who have not yet heard the gospel message. Larry has been overwhelmed by the grace of God that he and the team have experienced for more than 20 years.

Larry has written more than 30 books, with over 500,000 copies in print. His books have been translated into more than ten languages. He and his wife, LaVerne, have been married for 39 years, and they have been blessed with four children and three grandchildren. Larry and LaVerne live in Lititz, Pennsylvania.

Jimmy Seibert is passionate and zealous about loving God and making Him known in all the earth. Throughout his humble journey of simple devotion and obedience, he and those who have served with him have been overwhelmed by the Lord's faithfulness, goodness and power. The result: Antioch Community Church in Waco, Texas—a church that is touching and changing the world for the kingdom of God.

Jimmy is the senior pastor of Antioch Community Church and founder and president of Antioch Ministries International (AMI). He has been involved in training and sending church planters for 21 years and has seen hundreds sent to the mission field. His desire is to see the local church own the vision of establishing churches throughout the earth. Jimmy and his wife, Laura, have been married for more than 20 years and have four children.

Jimmy has written the book *The Church Can Change the World*, which reads like an extension of the book of Acts—telling the stories of men and women committed to the gospel, no matter the cost, and of God's miraculous presence infusing their steps with effectiveness. Jimmy says, "God wants to be known in all the earth. He wants to rightly distribute Himself so that all can hear and all can know. The way He has chosen to do that is through the Church. We follow in the footsteps of thousands who have gone before us, but this is our time. It is our hour to see the coming of the Lord—to be a part of God's dream by answering His heart's cry."

Resources from DOVE International (DCFI)

Building Your Personal House of Prayer
by Larry Kreider
254 pages, $15.99, ISBN 978-0-7684-2662-5

If you love to pray, or you need to pray more effectively, this book will change your prayer life forever. Your entire approach to prayer is about to improve! Imagine eagerly awaiting your prayer time, praying with confidence, and having your heart full of faith as you commune with God. This book is a gold mine of tools you need to have the prayer life you know you want and need.

Speak Lord, I'm Listening
by Larry Kreider
224 pages, $14.99, ISBN 978-0-830746-12-5

Jesus said, "My sheep hear My voice," but many Christians do not know how to hear from God. In this practical, story-rich guidebook, international teacher Larry Kreider shows believers how to develop a listening relationship with the Lord. Larry explores the multiple ways Christians can hear the voice of God in today's world, offering real-life examples—not theory—of how God teaches His followers to listen, with tips in each chapter for distinguishing His voice from the noise of Satan's interference. Christians across the denominational spectrum will develop a closer and deeper relationship with God as they learn 50 unique ways to listen to Him. You will realize that God was speaking to you all along but, like the disciples on the road to Emmaus, you didn't know it was Him!

Hearing God: 30 Different Ways
by Larry Kreider
224 pages, $14.99, ISBN 978-1-886973-76-3
The Lord speaks to us in ways we often miss, including
through the Bible, prayer, circumstances, spiritual gifts,
conviction, His character, His peace, and even in times
of silence. Take 30 days and discover how God's voice
can become familiar to you as you develop a loving
relationship with Him.

The Cry for Spiritual Fathers & Mothers
by Larry Kreider
186 pages: $12.99, ISBN: 978-1-886973-42-8
Returning to the biblical truth of spiritual parenting so that
believers are not left fatherless and disconnected. How loving,
seasoned spiritual fathers and mothers help spiritual children
reach their potential.

The Biblical Role of Elders for Today's Church
by Larry Kreider, Ron Myer, Steve Prokopchak, and Brian Sauder
274 pages: $12.99, ISBN: 978-1-886973-62-6
New Testament principles for equipping church leadership
teams: Why leadership is needed, what their qualifications
and responsibilities are, how they should be chosen, how elders function as spiritual fathers and mothers, how they are to
make decisions and resolve conflicts, and more.

Biblical Foundations for Your Life Series:
Discovering the Basic Truths of Christianity
by Larry Kreider
199 pages, $17.99, ISBN 978-0-768427-48-6

Building Your Life on the Basic Truths of Christianity
by Larry Kreider
199 pages, $17.99, ISBN 978-0-768427-49-3
This two-book series by Larry Kreider covers basic Christian doctrine. Practical illustrations accompany the easy-to-understand format. Use for small-group teachings (48 in all), a mentoring relationship or a daily devotional.

Authentic Spiritual Mentoring
by Larry Kreider
224 pages, $14.99, ISBN: 978-0-8307-4413-8
In this book, Larry Kreider offers proven biblical keys that will open the door to thriving mentoring relationships. You will learn the Jesus Model of mentoring—initiate, build and release—and how to apply it to the spiritual family God is preparing for you. Whether you are looking for a spiritual mentor or desiring to become one, this book is for you!

Growing the Fruit of the Spirit
by Larry Kreider and Sam Smucker
160 pages, $14.99, ISBN978-1-886973-93-0
This book encourages you to check your spiritual health and wellness to see if you are exhibiting the nine characteristics described in Galatians 5:22-23 as the fruit of the Spirit.

Helping You Build Cell Churches
A training manual compiled by Brian Sauder and Larry Kreider
224 pages, $19.95, ISBN 978-1-886973-38-1
A complete biblical blueprint for small groups, this manual covers 51 topics! Includes study and discussion questions. Use for training small-group leaders or personal study.

Church Planting and Leadership Training
(Live or Video School with Larry Kreider and Others)

The purpose of this school is to train the leaders our world is desperately looking for. We provide practical information as well as Holy Spirit-empowered impartation and activation. Be transformed and prepared for a lifetime of ministry and service to others.

If you know where you are called to serve—church, small group, business, public service, marketplace—or simply want to grow in your leadership ability, our goal is to help you build a biblical foundation to be led by the Holy Spirit and pursue your God-given dreams. For a complete list of classes and venues, visit www.dcfi.org.

School of Global Transformation
Seven-month Residential Discipleship School

Be equipped for a lifetime of service in the Church, marketplace and beyond! The School of Global Transformation is a seven-month residential discipleship school that runs September through March. Take seven months to satisfy your hunger for more of God. Experience His love in a deeper way than you ever dreamed possible. He has a distinctive plan and purpose for your life. We are committed to helping students discover destiny in Him and preparing them to transform the world around them. For details, visit www.dcfi.org.

Seminars

One-day seminars with Larry Kreider and other DOVE Christian Fellowship International authors and leaders:

How to Build Small Groups: Basic
How to Grow Small Groups: Advanced

How to Fulfill Your Calling as a Spiritual Father or Mother
21 Tests of Effective Leadership
Planting Churches Made Practical
Counseling Basics
Starting House Churches
Effective Fivefold Ministry Made Practical
Building Your Personal House of Prayer
How to Build Healthy Leadership Teams
How to Hear God 30 Different Ways
Called Together Couple Mentoring
How to Live in Kingdom Prosperity
How to Equip and Release the Prophetic Ministry

For more information about DCFI seminars, Call: 800-848-5892
Email: seminars@dcfi.org

Author Contact
Larry Kreider, International Director,
DOVE Christian Fellowship International

11 Toll Gate Road
Lititz, PA 17543
Tel: 717-627-1996
Fax: 717-627-4004
www.dcfi.org
LarryK@dcfi.org

Resources from Antioch Community Church

Books

The Church Can Change the World
Ignite: The Birth of a Church Planting Movement
Impact: Leading Short Term Trips for Long Term Impact
From Venus to Mars and Back: What It Means to be You
God of the Impossible: The Healing of Anna Joy

Devotional Books for Families

It's All Grace
Joyful (book and flip calendar)
Who God Says I Am

You can find these resources and more at
www.antiochcc.net

ALSO BY
LARRY KREIDER

**What Every Small-Group
Leader Should Know**
ISBN 978.08307.53277

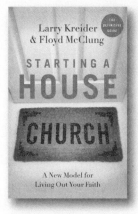

Starting a House Church
(with Floyd McClung)
ISBN 978.08307.43650

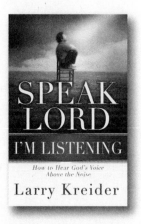

Speak, Lord, I'm Listening
ISBN 978.08307.46125

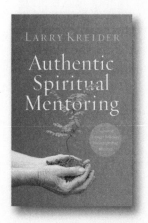

Authentic Spiritual Mentoring
ISBN 978.08307.44138

Available at Bookstores Everywhere!

Go to **www.regalbooks.com** to learn more about your
favorite Regal books and authors. Visit us online today!

Regal
God's Word for Your World™
www.regalbooks.com